big city drop-outs

and
illiterates

Robert A. Dentler

Mary Ellen Warshauer

center for urban education
1965

379.240973
D414b

A Study of Educational Barriers to Economic Security
under a Grant (Number 148) from the Social Security
Administration, United States Department of Health,
Education, and Welfare.

The research and development reported herein
was performed pursuant to a contract with the
United States Department of Health, Education,
and Welfare, Office of Education, under the
provisions of the Cooperative Research Program.

TO

E. W. Burgess, Pioneer

CONTENTS

List of Tables

Table

PREFACE

THE COMPARATIVE ANALYSIS of characteristics of large cities, which constitutes the heart of this book, is an established tradition in American social science. In 1937, William F. Ogburn published his now virtually forgotten yet still pertinent monograph, *Social Characteristics of Cities*. Edward Thorndike followed with *Your City*, in 1939, and *144 Smaller Cities*, in 1940. Robert Cooley Angell extended the tradition with *The Moral Integration of American Cities*, in 1951, and more recently, Otis Dudley Duncan and Albert J. Reiss, Jr., improved on the heritage with *Social Characteristics of Urban and Rural Communities*. Otis Duncan, Richard W. Scott, Stanley Lieberson, Beverly Duncan, and Hal H. Winsborough followed with *Metropolis and Region*, in 1960. A new line of analysis within the tradition was revealed in *American Cities: Their Social Characteristics* by Edgar F. Borgatta and Jeffrey K. Hadden, in 1965.

Ogburn's major concern was to show how size, region, growth or decline, and specialization are correlated with social trends within cities. He sampled 434 cities, collecting a wealth of information on population traits, occupational structure, family life, social services, housing, leisure, and trade. The data were presented only according to size categories, in bar graphs and in simple percentages. Moreover, Ogburn made no mention of which cities he was studying. Yet his study was monumental in that it was one of the first attempts to examine systematically differences across a large sample of cities.

Thorndike tried to determine what makes a city a "good place" in which to live. In his first book, he studied 310 of the largest cities in

ix

the United States; he supplemented this analysis with additional information on 144 smaller cities in his second book. He gathered data
on approximately 300 different items ranging from latitude and longi-
tude, per capita domestic installations of telephones, and per capita
circulation of *Modern Screen, Radio Stars,* and *Modern Romances,* to
per capita expenditures on health, school, recreation and parks, and
a wealth of social, economic, and occupational characteristics. Thorndike extended Ogburn's statistical design. He constructed three in-
dexes and computed zero order correlations.

Angell utilized a very limited number of variables in his study of
''moral integration'' in 43 of the larger cities in the country. His
statistical design, however, included multiple correlation analysis,
simple index construction, and questionnaire and interview material
obtained in four communities.

Our study follows directly the line of comparative analysis begun
by Ogburn and utilized by many others since. Although, today, this
approach is filled with theoretical as well as methodological traps,
we feel that it is still useful. The contribution of our study to the
comparative tradition can possibly be viewed as twofold. First is
our use of multiple regression analysis as an organizing rather than
a predicting procedure. Secondly, we have tried to bring this comparative analytical tradition to bear upon contemporary indicators
of importance to national policy in planning for both economic security and educational development.

We began this study in 1963 under a research grant from the United
States Social Security Administration. At that time, the relation between economic insecurity and low educational attainment was a widely
advertised condition. Programs to prevent withdrawal from high
school or to rehabilitate dropouts, and programs to educate adult illiterates were burgeoning in cities throughout the United States.

Accordingly, we wanted to devise a way of *ranking* metropolitan
communities in terms of their ''production'' of high school dropouts
and adult illiterates, in the conviction that social and educational programs should proceed from a clear description of similarities and
differences among localities. We were further convinced that a meaningful ranking of communities should involve comparisons that took
economic, demographic, and other social differences between cities
into account.

Our policy interests went a step beyond this descriptive goal. We
also wanted to see whether relative differences in dropouts and in
adult illiterates among cities were associated with selected features
of the local economy and social structure. We were also interested
in a comparative analysis of the effects of programs to prevent or to
rehabilitate dropouts and illiterates.

Thus, we sought to answer three related questions: Can we devise
indicators of the relative performance of big cities with respect to two

kinds of educational characteristics? When differences due to social and economic background conditions are held constant statistically, what are the correlates of high school withdrawal and adult functional illiteracy? And, how are efforts to develop educational or social programs related to community characteristics?

In our judgment, the study's results broaden knowledge of the relationship between educational attainment and economic insecurity. This is particularly the case insofar as programs in the future may be designed in terms of community rather than individual or family situations. Our results also suggest to us that national and state economic policies, including programs of social insurance, may be of substantial importance in fostering increased educational attainment, while school and welfare programs that attempt to deal *directly* with dropout prevention or literacy are irrelevant if not futile.

We are grateful for the help of Don Pilcher and Phillips Cutright of the United States Social Security Administration, and to James Cowhig of the United States Welfare Administration. All three read a draft of our manuscript and made helpful suggestions. Sociologists Donnell Pappenfort and Stanley Lieberson also offered comments on portions of our work. Rosedith Sitgreaves and Neil Henry provided us with valuable statistical guidance.

Our colleague, the late Theresa M. Barmack, gave continual support to this inquiry, in project administration, manuscript preparation, and above all, in warm encouragement. We thank Marcia Hyman and Winifred Meskus for their assistance in preparing drafts of the manuscript, and we acknowledge the diligence and skill of George Yonemura, who assisted us in data preparation and processing. Richard P. Boardman gave us informed guidance in utilizing the computer.

This study could not have been conducted without the cooperation of the United States Bureau of the Census, who supplied us with special tabulations. We are most grateful for the voluntary responses of dozens of city and state school and welfare officers, who provided information about special education and welfare programs. We hope they will find something of intellectual or practical value in this report.

ROBERT A. DENTLER
MARY ELLEN WARSHAUER

New York City, 1965

CHAPTER 1

DIMENSIONS
OF THE PROBLEM

BASES OF ECONOMIC SECURITY

IN the United States, such credentials of schooling as diplomas and number of years completed have long been important in affecting a person's job and income prospects. Since World War II, the symbols of education have become crucial. In 1959, adult workers with eighth grade diplomas earned $3,600 a year on the average. Those who went on to high school but withdrew before graduating earned about $4,300. High school graduates earned about $4,800 on the average that year. The greatest gap falls between the income of college graduates and everyone else, suggesting that in the near future not even the high school diploma will offer much work and income security. Meanwhile, we are certain that the conditions of unemployment, underemployment, unstable prospects in the job market, and ineffectual drifting across jobs, are all strongly correlated with withdrawal from high school or junior high.

The relation of limited education to job insecurity and thus to welfare dependency is ubiquitous, but it is especially noteworthy in large cities. The Cook County (Illinois) Department of Welfare found, in an analysis of General Assistance applications for a six week period in 1959, for example, that:

> Despite indications of economic recovery, unemployment was the primary cause for these applications. Thus, 70.7 percent of the applications could be attributed either directly or indirectly, to unemployment and not

1

to social, psychological or physical factors. . . . The main characteristics
these persons had in common were low levels of education and low levels
of training. . . . 88.4 percent had not completed high school and. . . 75.2
fell into the unskilled classification. (Brooks, 1962, p. 1)

Although low educational attainment is linked with unemployment and underemployment generally, it is in the city that this relation becomes most dramatic. The uneducated city dweller is consign-
ed to low level employment at low wages, or increasingly, to permanent unemployment. Prior to World War I, adult illiteracy was con-
centrated in rural populations and in seaport cities receiving large
numbers of European immigrants. For the rural populations, however, the effects of adult illiteracy were somewhat less detrimen-
tal to family and individual security. The new order of deprivation,
however, is mainly urban and it is an outgrowth of rural migration.
As the city-wide migration of deprived households persists, central
cities are affected to the extent that adult illiteracy contributes to
the transmission of educational disadvantages, to the lowering of pro-
ductivity, and to the reduction of the flow of consumer goods. Big city
economies have changed from dependence upon cheap, abundant, unskilled labor to increasing dependence upon technical skills and job
flexibility, two abilities correlated with literacy and with level of
formal education.

POLICY CONCERN WITH DROPOUTS

IT is against the background of these and other social, economic, and
educational changes, that welfarists and educators have asserted
more and more emphatically since World War II that the problem of
finding ways to encourage youths to complete high school is one of
the most crucial current issues in American society. The message
has been repeated so emphatically that the government has invested
in programs to rescue former dropouts and to rehabilitate potential
ones. The mass media have joined in, for the most part on the basis
of tax-deductible advertising, to campaign for a return to high school.
Social agencies have contributed an array of diagnostic examinations,
casework and groupwork services, and clinical orientations that have
helped to foster an image of The Dropout as a special type of character disorder.

Is, however, withdrawal from high school actually a crucial issue?
What aspects of the evidence are sometimes neglected? Is The Dropout perhaps a gloss for a more fundamental policy problem—the in-
tensifying underemployment of youth? This study explores these
questions in the spirit of the policy scientist. The evidence and its
interpretation are fitted to the larger forces of automation and ur-
banization in order to articulate a broader, more fundamental chal-
lenge than school withdrawal.

Neglected Evidence

AN educational problem is first of all a matter of definition. Policy makers and educational practitioners concerned with school withdrawal like to fashion their rhetoric so that the extent of withdrawal seems large. They typically report that about one out of two children who begin elementary school in the United States finishes high school, and that only half of those who finish high school go on to college. On the surface, this is not too far from the facts. For every 1,000 students enrolled in fifth grade in 1951, 582 graduated from high school by 1959, and 308 of this group entered college.

But this is only the surface. First, it is worthwhile to treat the rate of withdrawal comparatively. If we look at fifth grade cohorts from 1920 through the present, and if we plot the dropout rate for each year, we obtain a rather smooth curve that shows a decline from about 80 percent high school withdrawal in 1920 to about 40 percent in 1960. If we follow the line of the resulting curve, we get the definite impression that in 1975, about thirty students per 100 will fail to graduate from high school, and that this number may drop to 20 percent by the end of the century. The historical evidence thus shows a pattern of eight decades of increasing levels of school retention, with a dramatic shift from an 80 percent likelihood of withdrawal from high school to an 80 percent likelihood of graduation.

This is still the surface. The dwindling fraction of those who drop out of school reveals some sizeable groups whose characteristics are obscured by the gross figures. There are students who change communities and schools without adequate transmission of records. There are mortalities, severe physical disabilities, and late-blooming mental retardates, as well as youth who suffer conditions defined as emotional disturbance and delinquency. These categories are extremely difficult to locate and measure. But if we follow the lead of researchers who have struggled to distinguish between voluntary and involuntary withdrawal on these bases, the rate of school withdrawal is reduced further. Applying the crude estimates of one of the best of these studies, it appears that voluntary withdrawal has declined from about 70 percent in 1920 to about 25 percent in 1960. A projection of this curve shows that the voluntary dropout rate should level off more or less permanently at about 15 percent by 1975.[1] This decline might be slightly over-estimated since there are other demographic forces such as the reduction in youth mortality, which might lessen the decline in withdrawal.

---

[1]Our data are drawn principally from tables in *Annual Health, Education and Welfare Trends, 1961* (U.S. Department of Health, Education and Welfare, 1962). For a careful treatment of the question of involuntary versus voluntary withdrawals, see Segal and Schwarm (1957).

Those who argue that the dropout is a major national educational problem also neglect the question of absolute numbers. For example, we are seldom reminded that the high-school-age population expanded 500 percent between 1920 and 1960. It will probably increase by another 400 percent between 1960 and 1975. The historical statistics suggest that the *number* of high school dropouts has remained relatively constant. For the period 1900 to 1950, the number averaged about 600,000 annually. Since then, the yearly crop of high school dropouts has hovered in the range of 650,000. This absolute increase is very slight if our baseline is the absolute number of high school age youths.

Mobility and Concern

FINALLY, those most concerned to promote new policies and practices for retaining youths in school tend to neglect the fluidity common to all communal, institutional, and occupational aspects of American life. We are seldom told, for example, that a dropout rate is usually based on a fifth grade cohort examined eight years later. Census data reveal the substantial number of persons aged 19 to 24 attending junior high schools and high schools, especially in metropolitan communities. For example, in New York City 25,239 people of this age are in junior and senior high schools. The comparable figures for Los Angeles and Detroit are, respectively, 7,527 and 5,641. There are many who remain in school but take additional years to graduate. A recent survey in Syracuse revealed, as one aspect of this neglected pattern, that 10 percent of all 1959-1960 high school dropouts returned to school to work toward graduation within the next two years. Another 15 percent sought further educational instruction of other sorts in the same period (Saleem & Miller, 1963).

The evidence suggests that, for the individual American student, the probability of graduating from high school has increased substantially during each decade. This improvement reflects the evolution of an educational system whose capabilities correspond to the requirements of rapid technological change and population growth. Much of the improvement, however, has resulted from changes in school promotion policies from a rule of success or failure grade-by-grade to a practice of social or age promotion. In turn, this change in policy is perhaps the glove on the fist of state laws prohibiting "premature" withdrawal from school and, most especially, the implementation of these laws. This increased probability of graduating may be a mixed blessing, but surely one cannot have matters both ways. A legally sanctioned system designed to keep most youths in school for the longest feasible period is bound to alienate some youths in the process.

In the sizeable literature about school dropouts, there seem to be three main genres. One genre is exhortative and hence of no concern to this research. A second group consists of descriptive statistical reports about dropout rates for regions, states, school districts, and particular communities. These would be valuable if some uniform and valid method could be developed that would allow confidence in the statements about parameters. The United States Office of Education and various agencies and institutions are now struggling to achieve this uniformity.

None of the literature is explicit about assumptions, theoretical or normative, but the third group of papers — surveys of the social and educational characteristics of alleged dropouts — offers a point of departure. The characteristics reappear with such regularity in the various studies that one is invited to generalize. The evident recurrence may be spurious, however. Educational researchers may merely imitate one another's questions. Very few studies attend closely, for instance, to the characteristics of the schools or the instructional staffs which make up the context out of which the dropout emerges. Nor are social and psychological differences between hypothetical types of dropouts emphasized (Miller, Saleem & Bryce, 1964; Tannenbaum, 1965, in press).

DROPOUTS IN PROFILE

THE recurrent attributes common to high school dropouts are easy to catalogue. The modal dropout is a low school achiever, usually below grade level for his age. He is a member of a low-income family in which the parents have low educational attainment. He participates infrequently in the extra-curricular life of his student peers. Some studies strain toward greater depth in tapping these attributes. Clinically oriented researchers tend to find character disorders. They hedge toward delineation of a disease or disability syndrome. Sociologically oriented researchers tend to find disorganized families and associated evidence of poor early socialization. These emphases draw our attention away from the school, its program, and its staff and direct us toward developmental failures.

Given the high positive intercorrelations between low educational, occupational, and economic attainment of parents, racial minority group membership, and marital and family disorganization, we may lump the surface attributes of the dropout together and view him as *deprived*. This concept may have relevance for theories of cognitive and emotional development (although this remains an empirical question), but it raises new difficulties. For example, the dropout is not *culturally* deprived. The standard of culture advanced by the school is but one standard among many; and in our society, schools are supposed to buttress some degree of cultural pluralism. In the same sense, social deprivation is ambiguous.

If we work with the connotation of deprivation, we make better headway. We can then conclude that the high school dropout is *educationally disadvantaged*. If he wants to live by the rules of the school game, his chances are reduced by counterpressures from his home and his environment outside school. If he is uncertain about the merits of staying in high school and graduating, his "background" and the response of educators to their own internalized assumptions about that background may reduce his ability to remove that uncertainty. In this event, the disadvantaged student is one who is vulnerable to determination from without. Finally, if he defines himself as a dropout in advance of legal age for withdrawal, his self-definition can be selectively reinforced by home, neighborhood peers, and the school itself. The dropout is educationally disadvantaged because, at any one moment, his behavioral setting includes forces that constrain him to quit school. That setting contains self, family, peers, and the school.

The survey literature strongly supports the impression that the *relation* between disadvantage (socioeconomic, ethnic, and — reciprocally — school experience) and voluntary withdrawal from school was as marked in 1928 as it was in 1958. The psychosocial correlates of withdrawal are durable as well as strong and readily identifiable. Because of this, a specious sort of timelessness enters interpretations of the dropout. The correlation coefficients remain the same; therefore, the interpretation of the meaning of disadvantage goes unchanged.

Logic and Fact

SUPPOSE we exercise our logic and our knowledge of social trends. Let us assume that the proportion of economically impoverished American households has declined rather steadily since 1910, and that because of improvements in the organization of education and changes in laws affecting withdrawal, the high school dropout rate has declined just as steadily. Finally, let us assume that the correlation between the economic level of the household and withdrawal from high school remains high and constant.

The hypothetical data in Table 1-1 permit an examination of the effects of these assumptions. The logic in the results is clear. The overall chance of being both disadvantaged economically and of dropping out *declines* from .40 in 1940 to .25 in 1960 to .15 in 1980. More intriguing and disturbing is the logical conclusion that the likelihood of graduating if one is disadvantaged declines over time. From our imaginary data, hypothetically, low economic status was less handicapping in 1940 than in 1960 or 1980. Twenty percent of the total students were both of low status and graduates in 1940, in contrast to 15 percent in 1980.

The intent here is to amplify the demographic process. As the society changes economically and educationally, the dropout who is

Table 1-1
Hypothetical Cross-Tabulation of High School Graduates and Dropouts Versus Status[a]

Status	Dropout	Graduate	Total
	Year: 1940		
Low[b]	40	20	60
Other	0	40	40
Total	40	60	100
	Year: 1960		
Low	25	15	40
Other	0	60	60
Total	25	75	100
	Year: 1980		
Low	15	15	30
Other	0	70	70
Total	15	85	100

[a]Years chosen to illustrate changing trends in holding power of schools and in socioeconomic mobility in population. Figures reflect rates per 100.
[b]Taken as composite of sources of relative environmental deprivation, e.g., low income, educational attainment of parents.

economically disadvantaged becomes a clearer object for concern. When his numbers were relatively legion, he was understandably less visible. Surely these changes in the larger context induce changes in what it means to be a dropout in each decade. As the various probabilities change, and if they change in the directions suggested by the imaginary data, the dropout will become educationally more problematic. Similarly, the credentials of the high school graduate become less impressive. His diploma fails to command selective attention on the job market as it becomes common property.

It is in this sense that the research literature on the dropout is misplaced. Educational and psychological surveys are conducted on the one hand; population, income, and educational statistics accumulate on the other. But no one connects the individual with the society.

The literature and, therefore, the problem are fuzzily conceived in another way, too. The attributes that we characterize as a ''disadvantage'' are not only aspects of the same pattern of the stratification; they are a circular statement of what is involved in withdrawal

from school. They tell us that a socioeconomic disadvantage is the
equivalent of an educational disadvantage, which is in turn productive
of poor school performance, disinterest, and withdrawal.

EMPLOYMENT AND AUTOMATION

THE main key to socioeconomic advantage in our society is secure
employment. But is graduation from high school a key to membership in the labor force, let alone to secure employment? A sound
analysis of national survey data by the Bureau of Labor Statistics challenges the affirmative answer offered by most commentators on the
dropout question.

Keep in mind when examining Table 1-2 that the average national
adult level of unemployment from 1959 through 1961 was about six
percent. Young adults who graduated from high school between 1955
and 1958 were generally employed by at least the fall of 1961. White
young adults in this group achieved an employment level identical to
the entire older national labor force. *White* young adult dropouts in
the same cohort were twice as likely to be unemployed, yet their overall unemployment level of 11.9 percent is low when contrasted with
nonwhites. About 94 percent of the white graduates, compared with
88 percent of the white dropouts, were employed.

There is an evident occupational handicap involved in dropping out,
but the handicap of race, of being nonwhite, is far greater. About 12
percent of the white *dropouts* were unemployed among those who had

Table 1-2
Job Fates of Recent High School Graduates and Dropouts, Excluding Those
Continuing School, by Color[a]

	Percent Unemployed in 1961 (Oct.) Among Graduates				Percent Unemployed in 1961 (Oct.) Among Dropouts		
Year Last in School[b]	Total	White	Non-white	Year Last in School[b]	Total	White	Non-white
Prior to 1959	7.4	6.3	17.8	Prior to 1959	12.7	11.9	15.5[c]
1959	8.3	7.2	16.7	1959	17.0	16.5	18.4
1960	11.6	11.0	17.9	1960	17.2	16.1	21.4
1961	17.9	16.3	31.0[c]	1961	26.8	29.1	18.0

[a]Adapted from Jacob Schiffman, (1962), especially detailed Tables A
and B.
[b]Data are from three-year panel survey of youths 16 to 24.
[c]Small-base N makes percent *less* reliable in these cells.

a few years to secure work, but nearly 18 percent of the nonwhite *graduates* in the same age group remained unemployed. Racial "minorityship" is a correlate of socioeconomic disadvantage. Thus, a high school diploma is a further economic advantage to those who have the socioeconomic advantage in the first place. It has little apparent job benefit to offer the youth stigmatized through discrimination.

The data in Table 1-2 suggest something else. Each year, most high school graduates and dropouts manage to find a way, however limited, into the labor force. They get jobs, although for many there is a lag between age 17 and the year of first real employment. This lag is greater for the dropout. For graduates, unemployment rates decline within three years after high school to about the level common to the entire civilian labor force. But the major youth problem is neither socioeconomic disadvantage nor failure to obtain a high school diploma. *It is, rather, a steady breakdown in the absorption of the young non-college graduate into the work force* as a result of the upgrading of occupational requirements through automation and the relation of this change to changes in the young adult population.

LABOR FORCE IN FLUX

THE new growth of the labor force from 1960 to 1970 will be about 13 million, an increase of more than half over the net growth from 1950 to 1960. If we assume that new jobs are generated at the pace set during the last five years, unemployment will amount to about eight percent of the labor force by 1970 in contrast to six percent in 1960. Most of the increase in job seekers — more than 40 percent, at least (Clark, 1958) — will be due to increases in the number of young adults entering the labor market.

The President's Advisory Committee on Labor-Management Policy reported in 1962:

> It is clear that unemployment has resulted from displacement due to automation and technological change. It is impossible, with presently available data, to isolate that portion of present unemployment resulting from these causes. Whether such a displacement will be short-run depends to a considerable extent on our ability to anticipate and plan for programs involving technological change and to make better use of various mechanisms for retraining and relocating workers who find themselves unneeded....

The absolute number of high school dropouts will probably remain fairly constant, even across the coming period of expansion of the young adult population, because of the increased rate of school retention. But the total number of young adults will increase so markedly over the next decade that competition among non-college graduates trying to enter the labor force in any capacity will prove to be more severe than in any recent period except for the Great Depression. Against this backdrop, high school graduation or the failure to graduate *will not* differentiate the employed from the unemployed.[2]

The social and educational outcomes are those of incompatible rates of change between technology and the occupational structure, or between automation (broadly conceived) and structural unemployment. The dropout rate is pertinent, but it has in fact declined steadily while more pertinent factors have not kept pace with the change in technology.[3]

Within education, adjustment to changing rates of automation is complicated by our inability to articulate general education prior to job training with changing work requirements. Ancillary educational enterprises in adult education, vocational preparation, and career counseling have often lacked fiscal support, and when they have secured support, they have failed to cope adequately with the tremendous complexities inherent in massive, rapid change. We have, for example, only begun to learn how to "retrain" young adults from unskilled to technically skilled workers.

The dimensions of reorganizing education have been well explored for years. While the discussion goes on, considerable slack is taken up outside schools by industry and government, where employers have the resources to train, to counsel, and to retrain individuals when the need for net returns dictates the importance of "classrooms in the factory" (Clark, 1958).

CENTRAL CITY LEVERAGE

Is there a *root* educational task in this thicket of changes and strains, however? Can priorities be assigned, not against a moral standard, but in terms of adaptations between institutions? The main root perhaps is the predominant response within education—increased holding power in higher education as well as in high school. The energies of the educational establishment have been invested for decades in

---

[2]Our argument rests on the premise of no substantial change in the rate of national economic growth. With increased growth and prosperity, automation could generate new employment in the ten-year short-term as it does in any case in the long-term.

[3]Among the noneducational factors of this problem, one might give priority to insufficient economic growth, periodic recessions, imbalance in economic changes from area to area with resulting chronic distress in some localities, limitations on labor force mobility, and incompletely developed and far from adequate unemployment insurance and related social security provisions—all, of course, in relation to rapid population growth.

widening the base for higher education. Thus (using the indicator of fifth grader cohorts), the rate of entry into college increased from twelve students per 100 in 1931 to thirty-two per 100 in 1960.

A prior task involves the residual group of youth from low status backgrounds, the dropouts and the high school graduates who do not enroll in school beyond the twelfth grade. For the generation current-ly in elementary and secondary schools, we have little to offer beyond remediation and retraining. Current federal proposals involve pri-marily only vocational training and make-work programs through up-dated, probably worthwhile variants of the Conservation Corps of the Great Depression.

A positive program for the non-college and the disadvantaged group must be stronger tactically and more transformative than this effort, however. The best possible point of departure is the search for ex-cellence in early instruction in *central city* schools.

The youth problem that is symbolized so superficially by the drop-out issue comes to a head in the central cities. The low-income fam-ilies, the rural households from the Deep South and the distressed areas of the mountain states, the racial minorities, and the small-town families of low educational attainment—all will continue their massive relocation into the nation's biggest central cities during the next fifteen years. Underemployment on the surplus of marginal farms, dwindling sources of rural nonfarm employment for unskilled workers, intensified conflict between racial groups in the South, and many other social and industrial forces continue to stimulate this old but inten-sifying movement.

Moreover, sociologists have recently verified their suspicion that earlier dichotomies between privileged suburban and deprived city families are breaking down as this cityward migration persists. For, in addition to growing numbers of lower status families in the *outer* ring of every large city, an increasing number of disadvantaged groups are beginning to cluster at points throughout the suburban and exurban but nonfarm areas beyond the city.

Cities initiate technological change; they are also highly vulnerable to its effects. Increasing unemployment and the under-employment of non-college educated youths will share in this dualism. Youth un-employment is already felt most sharply in the larger cities. The transformative capability of metropolitan communities lies in their ability to muster skills and to foster action. In this case, we think the main attack should be on *improvement in the quality of early gen-eral elementary education.*

ADULT ILLITERACY

THE matter of low educational attainment or what is often called func-tional illiteracy among adults has also become a major concern of some welfarists and educators. Civilian labor force members under twenty-five years of age will account for nearly half of the total growth in the labor force during the present decade, but there will also be a 20 percent increase in workers forty-five years of age and over. Among this group, and among the substantial number of unemployed and under-employed workers between twenty-five and forty-four years of age, il-literacy, or the functional equivalent of less than five years of school, constitutes a substantial barrier to income and job security.

Many of the nation's large cities maintain programs of basic educa-tion for adults, and the content of many of these programs reveals a sharp awareness among educators of the relation between schooling and economic security. A few of these programs have shown that con-certed efforts can be effective, although work with functional illiter-ates has not gone beyond demonstrations and pilot projects in any save the largest cities.

For example, the Department of Welfare in Cook County, Illinois demonstrated in 1962 that adult welfare recipients could improve their employability and earning capacity through basic instruction in reading. A project in Atlanta, Georgia, combined basic reading instruc-tion with job training for mothers receiving support under the Aid-to-Dependent-Children program. In New Haven, Syracuse, Boston, and New York City, community action programs have developed promis-ing pilot projects that bring relevant educational services to function-ally illiterate adults.

These welfare-oriented educational programs in large cities will doubtless spread during the next five years. Before they are intro-duced widely, however, and perhaps before efforts to evaluate them are attempted, we should conduct research that describes, compares, and explains the educational characteristics of urban populations in terms of the relevant social and economic correlates.

For example, some Federal programs of aid for depressed areas — foreign as well as domestic — operate through analytical procedures for classifying applicant areas, communities, or regions as "major," "smaller," or "very small." Here, measures have been devised for assessing the degree and extent of distress of the depressed area *in relation* to conditions in the surrounding region. Southern Appalachia may be absolutely depressed, but work toward elimination of depres-sion there requires knowledge of the level of depression relative to comparable areas in the national society and economy.

ORGANIZING HYPOTHESES OF STUDY

FOR reasons advanced at several points throughout this first chapter, we have elected to concentrate upon the *context* of insecurity, rather than upon the individual or family characteristics associated with low educational attainment or with welfare dependency. In case this

rather peculiar emphasis is still ambiguous, we cite a few analogies.
Kenneth Boulding stated, for example:

> Poverty is not a condition of the individual person, but is always a con-
> dition of a society or of a sub-culture within a society.... A poor relation
> in a rich family is in a different position than the poor man who has no rich
> relations. Their psychology is different and their whole style of life and
> consumption is likely to be different. (Boulding, 1961)

It is in this same sense that it is one thing to be a poor migrant
worker who accurately anticipates a good berry crop to be harvested,
and another thing entirely to be a poor migrant worker who accurately anticipates a poor crop or a struggle to find fair wages in a state
with poorly enforced regulations of work terms. Our aim has been to
reverse this conception of context and apply it to levels of educational attainment characteristic of whole cities.

Our major organizing and working hypothesis has been: differences in levels of high school withdrawal and of adult functional illiteracy in large cities are *functions* of differences in urban community
population composition, size, and change, and of differences in occupational structure, personal income, and employment conditions. In
other words, we have tested the hypothesis that while a myriad of individual choices and dispositions influence the individual decision to
withdraw from high school, these choices and dispositions are made
within an equally determinative context of life prospects. The *context of life prospects,* as we view it, is most often and most objec-
tively reflected in indicators of growth, wealth, and employment.

This hypothesis is more pertinent to the dropout rate than to adult
illiteracy. Low adult educational attainment is a social fact that reflects *prior* historical conditions. In one respect, the percent of adults
with less than fifth grade education may have no more relation to the
current socioeconomic prospects or conditions of cities than some
variable that is equally descriptive, yet historical, such as percent of
adults who had whooping cough as infants. Notice, however, that our
organizing hypothesis is not *causal* in the narrow sense. We are interested in the multiple correlates of two educational barriers to income and job security. One of these is static, hence its correlates
may not be viewed readily as determinants. The other — dropout
rate — may properly be conceived as an outcome of a community
context.

Our minor working hypothesis has been: departures of cities from
levels of school withdrawal and adult illiteracy as predicted from the
best multiple regression equations obtained in testing our major
hypothesis are *functions* of differences in municipal expenditures for
health, education, and welfare services. Here, our hypothesis suggests
that a city with a *lower* dropout rate than would be expected from the

regression analysis is probably a city where program or service activities — as reflected in expenditures — compensate for, and thus serve to reduce the barrier to security implicit in low educational attainment.

We anticipated great complications in examining these two hypotheses. Their purpose was principally to order our research procedures and interpretations, however. In the process, we intended to focus intensively on whatever pattern of empirical social and economic relationships could be identified through multiple regression analysis. The range of variables, their nature and limitations, and the full technical particulars concerning these procedures, are reported in Appendix A.

CHAPTER 2

EXPLAINING
DIFFERENCES
IN DROPOUT RATES

THIS chapter reports the findings of a study of high school dropout differences across 131 of the largest cities in the United States. Through multiple correlation and regression analysis, we have attempted to identify and analyze the social and economic correlates of withdrawal from high school in these cities. On the basis of our findings, we have classified the cities into three groups: those in which the dropout rates are identical with what we would expect in view of the city's social and economic conditions; those where the rates are higher; and those where they are lower than predicted. In this chapter we will also examine selected social and economic conditions in those communities that have rates which are much higher or lower than expected.[1]

The high school dropout rate for each city was computed by dividing the number of dropouts (persons *not* enrolled in school who had completed grades 8, 9, 10, or 11) by the "total population" (those enrolled in high school plus those not enrolled in school who had completed grades 8, 9, 10, or 11). The data were compiled for the population aged fourteen to nineteen. All data in this chapter, as well as the next, will be reported separately for the white and non-white populations.

---

[1]For a detailed discussion of our data collection procedure, specification of our dependent variable, and methodology, see Appendix A.

THE WHITE DROPOUT RATE

THE multiple correlation between the white dropout rate and selected
social and economic characteristics of the cities was R = .87. These
social and economic variables have, therefore, accounted for 76 percent of the possible variance in this dependent variable.

As Table 2-1 demonstrates, the principal factors in the equation,
and their relative contribution to the total predicted variance are:
percent of the labor force in white collar occupations (16%), percent
of white families with incomes under $1,000 (16%), the white adult
functional illiteracy rate (10%), percent of overcrowded housing
units (9%), percent of white families with incomes between $1,000 to
$1,999 (8%), percent of the population under five years of age (7%),
percent increase in the total population from 1950 to 1960 (6%), and
the nonwhite dropout rate (5%).

The variables thus differ in their relative contributions to total
predicted variance. Knowledge of the percentage of white collar
workers or the percent of white families with income under $1,000
provides the same relative understanding of the white dropout rate.
However, either one contributes about twice as much as that provided by age, and about three times as much as the insight gained
from variation in the nonwhite dropout rate. Similar comparative
statements could be made for the other independent components of
the regression equation.

In addition to differing in their relative contributions to total predicted variance, the variables show a different relationship to the
dependent variable. All but two have a positive relationship to the
white dropout rate. The exceptions are the percent in white collar
occupations and the percent increase in total population. This suggests that cities having *low* percentages of white collar workers,
low recent population increase, and *high* percentages of low income
families, illiterates, overcrowded housing units, population con-
centration (especially of children under five), and more nonwhite
dropouts compared to other cities, exhibit a higher white dropout
rate. On the whole, the pattern suggests the strong relationship between indicators of poverty and high white dropout rates.

Although the income and education variables refer to the extremes
of the continuum, the occupation variable does not. The negative relationship is not with the customary percentage of professionals, the
top extreme end of the continuum, but instead with a much broader
category. "White collar occupations" include professional, managerial (except farm), clerical, and sales workers. *On the whole,
therefore, a city with a very high white dropout rate, compared
to other cities, would be a disadvantaged community occupationally.*

A city which exhibits a low rate of population growth in comparison to other communities is generally stable and unchanging, or less

Table 2-1
Independent Components of White Dropout Regression and Their Contributions to Total Predicted Variance

Independent Components of Regression	Contributions		
	Beta	Zero Order r	Percent of Relative Contribution to Total Predicted Variance[a]
26.[b] Percent in White Collar Occupations	−0.3093	−.53	16%
14. Percent White Income Under $1,000	0.3119	.52	16
22. White Adult Illiteracy Rate	0.1922	.51	10
28. Percent Occupied Units with 1.01+ Per Room	0.2363	.39	9
15. Percent White Income Between $1,000-$1,999	0.2159	.39	8
12. Percent Population Under 5 Years	0.4086	.16	7
7. Percent Increase in Population 1950-1960	−0.1890	−.30	6
52. Nonwhite Dropout Rate	0.1167	.41	5
11. Nonworker Ratio	−0.3314	−.09	3
3. Total Population in 1960	0.0774	.25	2
41. Percent Males 35-44 Not in Labor Force	0.0803	.21	2
13. Percent Population Between 5-18 Years	−0.1190	−.09	1
34. Percent White Male Laborers	0.0308	.17	1
24. Percent White Unemployment	−0.1968	−.00	0
29. Percent White In-Migration	0.1199	−.14	−2[c]
8. Percent Negro in 1960	−0.2296	.35	−8[c]
	R = .87[d]		76%

[a]Column equals Beta value multiplied by Zero Order r. Total equals total predicted variance explained or R^2. This is true of all following tables.

[b]Numbers correspond to complete Variable Listing in Table B-1, Appendix B. This is true of all following tables.

[c]To arrive at R and R^2 when sign on Beta and Zero Order r differ, the variable must be subtracted from total predicted variance in accordance with the formula in Appendix A, page 84. True of all following tables.

[d]Significant at .01 level.

Table 2-2

Correlation Matrix of Major Variables Included in White Dropout Regression

Variables	26	14	22	28	15	12	7
14	−28						
22	−59	42					
28	−19	21	14				
15	−15	80	26	−01			
12	−05	−17	−10	62	−25		
7	42	−17	−43	31	−23	51	
52	−28	18	24	09	08	−03	−18

viable. Low population growth would mean low rates of in-migration compared to out-migration and low birth rates. In general, then, the given population would maintain itself. Suppose that a community were disadvantaged in the sense that its proportion of white collar workers was low, its percentage of low income families high, its level of educational achievement low, and its overcrowding high. Then the possibility of outside factors influencing or leading to change through in-migration would also be low. A low rate of population increase, given the related variables, fosters a high white dropout rate, for it helps to sustain the conditions that surround poverty.

At the same time, the presence of larger numbers of young children means additional pressures for support and subsistence in a relatively disadvantaged community. Poverty is more apt to be felt, less likely to be alleviated, and, given the other factors, conditions unfavorable to remaining in school are likely to be heightened.

In summary, those cities which are comparatively disadvantaged, demographically static communities, or communities with large populations of the very young, would exhibit higher white dropout rates than others.

THE NONWHITE DROPOUT RATE

THE multiple correlation between the nonwhite dropout rate and selected social and economic characteristics across the big cities is R = .67. The most meaningful combinations of independent variables account for 45 percent of the variance in nonwhite dropout rates. We were thus less successful in locating the factors related to the nonwhite dropout rate than the white.

Table 2-3
Independent Components of Nonwhite Dropout Regression and Their Contributions to Total Predicted Variance.

Independent Components of Regression		Contributions		
		Beta	Zero Order r	Percent of Relative Contributions to Total Predicted Variance[a]
51.[b]	White Dropout Rate	0.4651	.41	19%
36.	Percent Nonwhite Male Operatives	0.2308	.33	8
23.	Nonwhite Adult Illiteracy Rate	0.3138	.20	6
9.	Percent Nonwhite Non-Negro, 1960	−0.2318	−.27	6
21.	Percent Nonwhite Income $10,000 or More	−0.2805	−.16	4
11.	Nonworker Ratio	−0.2056	−.19	4
42.	Percent Nonwhite Female Dependency	0.1472	.19	3
38.	Percent Nonwhite Male Laborers	0.1274	.20	3
3.	Total Population, 1960	0.1391	.11	1
25.	Percent Nonwhite Unemployment	0.1226	.12	1
37.	Percent Nonwhite Male Service Workers	−0.0997	−.07	1
41.	Percent Males 35-44 Not in Labor Force	0.1065	.05	0
53.	Median Rent	0.2719	−.01	−0[c]
2.	Population Per Square Mile	−0.0829	.13	−1[c]
6.	Percent Nonwhite, 1950	−0.3213	.04	−1[c]
18.	Percent Nonwhite Income Under $1,000	−0.1733	.12	−2[c]
26.	Percent in White Collar Occupations	0.2644	−.28	−7[c]
		R = .67[d]		45%

[a]See Table 2-1, page 17.
[b]See Table 2-1.
[c]See Table 2-1.
[d]Significant at .01 level.

Table 2-4
Correlation Matrix of Major Variables Included in Nonwhite Dropout Regression

Variables	51	36	23	9	21
36	24				
23	26	31			
9	−22	−36	−41		
21	−09	10	−30	55	
11	−09	−02	28	−25	−24

As Table 2-3 shows, the principal factors in this equation and their relative contributions to total predicted variance are: the white dropout rate (19%), percent of nonwhite male operatives (8%), the nonwhite adult functional illiteracy rate (6%), percent of the population who are nonwhite and non-Negro (6%), percent of nonwhite families with incomes of $10,000 or more (4%), and the percent of non-workers (4%).

As in the white dropout regression, the variables differ in their relative contributions to total predicted variance. Knowledge of the level of the white dropout rate contributes twice as much understanding as that provided by the level of nonwhite operatives and almost five times as much as the understanding gained from looking at the percent of nonwhite families earning $10,000 or more,[2] or the non-worker ratio.

Comparison of the relative contributions of the variables in the white and nonwhite regressions yields some interesting results. There is a much wider spread in the nonwhite regression than in the white. In the latter, the first two variables had the same relative contribution to total predicted variance (16%) and these provided only three times as much as the last factor which added 5 percent. In the nonwhite regression the relative contribution of the first variable (19%) is higher than either major contributor on the white regression, and provides twice as much understanding as the second factor and five times as much as the last two variables.

In addition, the level of the nonwhite dropout rate added 5 percent to the total possible predicted variance in the white regression or 6 percent of the explained variance (see Table 2-1). The white dropout rate contributes 19 percent to the nonwhite regression or 42 percent

---

[2]Although we recognize the substantive difference between "earnings" and "income," our use of "earnings" throughout the book is synonymous with "income."

of the explained variance. Although the level of the nonwhite dropout rate has some influence on the white rate, this influence is small. However, the white dropout rate has a considerable influence on the percentage of nonwhites leaving school. Indeed, it accounts for 42 percent of the explained variance.

A similar comparative statement can be made concerning white versus nonwhite adult functional illiteracy levels. The relative influence of these variables in the white and nonwhite regressions are the same. The white illiteracy level adds 10 percent to the total possible predicted variance on the white regression which is 13 percent of the explained variance. The comparable figures for the nonwhite illiteracy level are 6 percent and 14 percent. Unlike the dropout rates, low adult educational attainment adds the same relative understanding of white and nonwhite withdrawal. With the exception of this variable, the factors associated with the white and nonwhite rates are different or of differing importance. Once again, the need to analyze this problem separately for the white and nonwhite populations has been reaffirmed.

In addition to differing in their relative contributions to total predicted variance, the variables show a different relationship to the dependent variable. Three of the factors have a positive relation to the nonwhite dropout rate, and three have a negative influence. Thus, cities having few high income nonwhite families, few nonworkers, and few nonwhite minority groups other than Negroes, and *high* percentages of nonwhite male operatives, adult illiterates, and white dropouts, compared to other cities, exhibit high nonwhite withdrawal rates. Cities in which the reverse pattern obtains would have a comparatively low percentage of nonwhite dropouts.

The components of this regression are different from those included in the white regression. In the first place, the negative influence of the percent of nonwhites who are not Negro on the dropout rate reaffirms once again the problems inherent in talking about the "nonwhite" population. As reference to Table 2-4 shows, the percent nonwhite non-Negro correlates positively with high nonwhite family income ($r = .55$) and negatively with nonwhite adult illiteracy ($r = -.41$). The non-Negro nonwhite population generally exhibits higher educational and occupational achievements than the Negro population. This is particularly true for Oriental groups. The inability to single out the Negro segment of the nonwhite population in this study might thus be the reason for the lower total variance (45%) explained on the nonwhite dropout rate.

On the whole, the major components of this regression do not show that impoverished conditions associate with a high nonwhite dropout rate. The reason for this may be that the nonwhite population is so severely and generally societally and economically disadvantaged to begin with. Their income, and occupational and educational attainment

are lower while their unemployment and dependency rates are higher.
Also, given the same educational background, a nonwhite person is
far less likely to obtain as good or as high paying a job as his white
counterpart.[3]

Since the nonwhite population is poorer, and has been exposed
over several generations to more extreme poverty than the white
population, disadvantaged conditions have less predictive bearing on
the nonwhite dropout rate than they do on the white rate.

Cities with higher white dropout rates and, correspondingly, more
depressed conditions present fewer avenues for betterment through
education. They also house higher numbers of *nonwhite* dropouts as
compared to other cities. When these conditions are reinforced by
high percentages of nonwhite operatives and illiterates in the adult
population and by *low* percentages of high income families and nonwhite non-Negroes in the population, a comparatively high nonwhite
withdrawal rate is maintained. The chances for improved security
through education are slight.

SUMMARY

IN the first part of this chapter we attempted to identify and analyze
the social and economic correlates of white and nonwhite withdrawal
from high school across 131 of the largest cities in the United States.
We were more successful in identifying the factors connected with
white withdrawal, but, as we indicated, the impossibility of separat-
ing the Negro population from other "nonwhites" in this study likely
accounts for the lower total variance explained on the nonwhite dropout rate. We have shown that different factors are accounting for
variations in these two rates, and that the white dropout rate is an important prediction of nonwhite withdrawal, while the reverse is not
true.

Finally, we have attempted to account for the reasons underlying

---

[3]The effect of the nonworker ratio on the nonwhite dropout rate is not
readily discernible. This variable represents the ratio of persons not in
the labor force, including children under fourteen, to those in the labor
force. In the light of the findings of both the white and nonwhite regressions, the expected influence of this variable was in a positive rather than
a negative direction. The lack of correlation between this variable and the
percent of males 35-44 not in the labor force ($r = .01$) and the correspondingly high correlation between the variable and the population between 5-18
($r = .59$) leads to the supposition that this variable might largely be a reflection of the young population in school and women who are mothers and
housewives. This variable can therefore be reflecting the incidence of
nonworking mothers and school attendance. Given both of these aspects,
the negative relationship between this variable and the nonwhite dropout
rate becomes self-explanatory.

the different relationships on these two regressions. Although the complete regression was presented, we limited our discussion to the major components of the regression—those accounting for most of the variance.[4]

White high school withdrawal was shown to be correlated (R = .87) with low levels of white collar workers and population increase, and high levels of low income families, adult illiteracy, overcrowded housing units, percent of young people under five, and nonwhite dropouts. These factors accounted for 76 percent of the possible variance on this dependent variable. Factors such as unemployment, population density, and median rent (which have been shown to have relative importance in other studies) add nothing to our account of the white dropout rate differences.

Nonwhite high school withdrawal was shown to be correlated (R = .67) with low incidence of high income families, nonworkers and nonwhite non-Negroes in the population, and high incidence of white dropouts, nonwhite operatives and adult illiterates. These factors accounted for 45 percent of the variance in the nonwhite dropout rate. Once again, the importance of unemployment, density, and median rent, was negligible.

DEVIANT CASE ANALYSIS

AS a result of the first stage of analysis, we were able to predict, in light of the correlated social and economic variables, white and nonwhite dropout rates for each of the cities. We then compared the actual and predicted rates, and classified the cities into three groups: those in which the dropout rates are identical, plus or minus one standard error, with what one would expect in view of the city's social and economic conditions; those where the rates are higher, and those where they are lower than predicted from the analysis. Figures 2-1 and 2-2 show the results of this procedure in graph form

Figure 2-1 shows the actual and predicted white dropout rates for the 131 cities. Figure 2-2 depicts the nonwhite rates. In both figures, the cities falling *within* the two diagonal lines are those in which the actual rates equal predicted rates, plus or minus one standard error. (The standard error for the white rates = 5.27; for the nonwhite rates, 8.05.) These cities were classified as predictable.

The cities having *higher actual* than predicted rates are located above the diagonal lines. Those with rates lower than predicted from the analysis are below the lines. These cities were termed deviant and labeled "above" and "below" respectively. The magnitude of the deviation can be judged by the distance from the line itself, which

---

[4]The reasons behind this decision can be found in Appendix A.

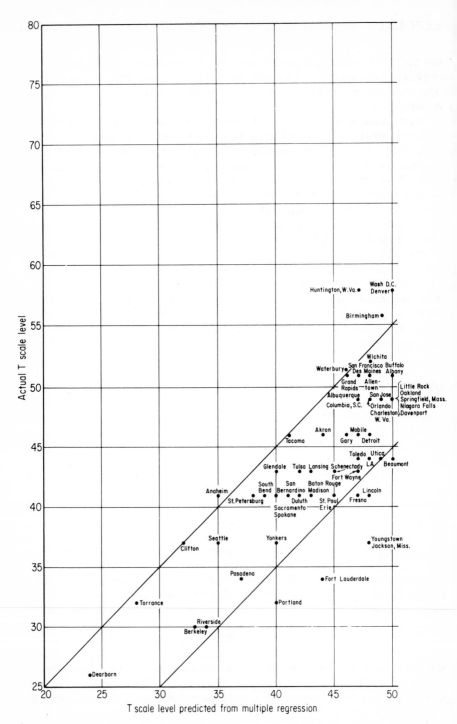

Figure 2-1
GRAPH OF T SCALE LEVEL OF WHITE DROPOUTS FOR 131 CITIES, BY
T SCALE LEVEL PREDICTED FROM MULTIPLE REGRESSION.*

24

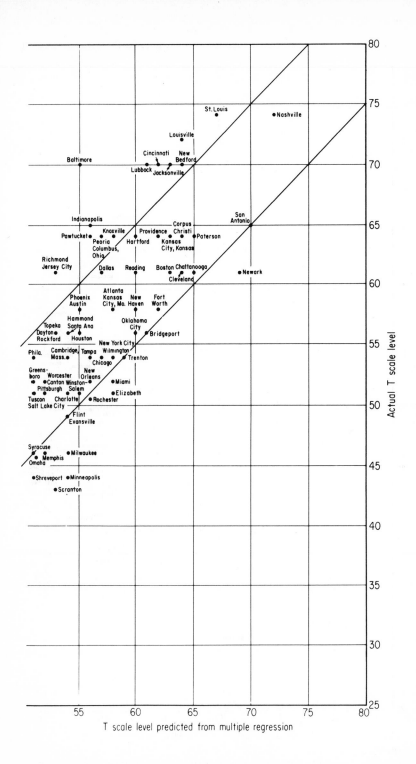

*From 1960 United States census data. Diagonal lines are error bands.

25

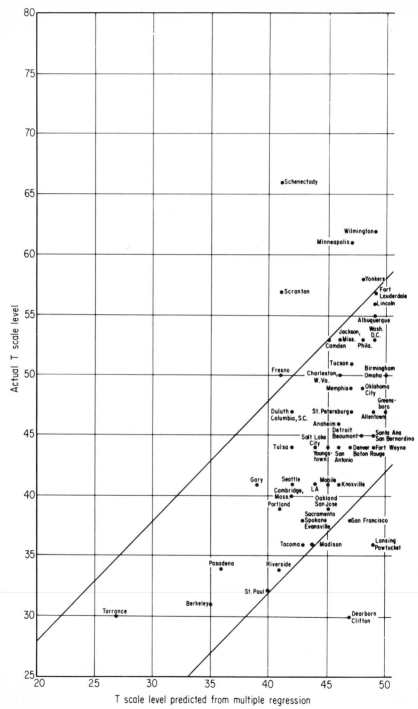

Figure 2-2
GRAPH OF T SCALE LEVEL OF NONWHITE DROPOUTS FOR 131 CITIES,
BY T SCALE LEVEL PREDICTED FROM MULTIPLE REGRESSION.*

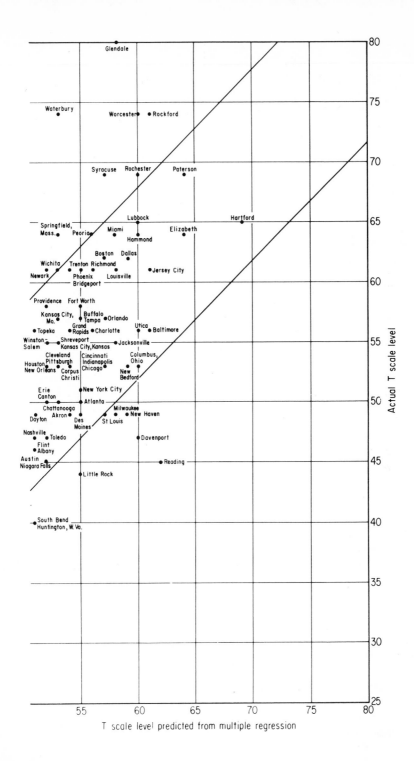

Actual T scale level

T scale level predicted from multiple regression

*From 1960 United States census data. Diagonal lines are error bands.

27

represents the difference between the actual and predicted rates. Baltimore and Schenectady show the highest "above" deviations on, respectively, the white and nonwhite regressions. This means that Baltimore has *more* white dropouts and Schenectady *more* nonwhite dropouts than expected.

Thirty-seven cities were classified as deviant on the white drop-out rate — twenty "above" and seventeen "below." Twenty-nine — sixteen "above" and thirteen "below" — were so labeled on the non-white rate. Eleven cities were deviant on both: Milwaukee, Water-bury, Peoria, Minneapolis, Newark, Rochester, Fresno, Scranton, St. Louis, Huntington (West Virginia), and Pawtucket. Milwaukee, Waterbury and Peoria are each deviant in the same direction on both rates — Milwaukee "below" and the other two "above." The next five cities mentioned are "below" on the white and "above" on the nonwhite. The last three show the reverse pattern.

The final stage of analysis was concerned with identifying and analyzing the social and economic conditions of the deviant cities. For this purpose, the "above" and "below" cities were singled out, and a separate analysis was done for each.[5]

Preliminary inspection of the nonwhite deviant cities caused us to eliminate five cities from this stage of analysis — Clifton, New Jersey; Dearborn, Michigan; Pawtucket, Rhode Island; Glendale, California; and Scranton, Pennsylvania — since the deviant status of these cities might have been a result of the data collection procedure employed due to their low levels of nonwhites. To prevent possible contami-nation of our results, we eliminated these five cities from the second stage of multiple correlation-regression analysis. In this second stage, the dependent variable became the residual, or the difference between the actual and predicted rates.

White Deviant Case Analysis

THE multiple correlation between the *white* residual and selected secondary variables was R = .50. The indicators of annual city expen-ditures and revenue, therefore, accounted for 25 percent of the possi-ble variance among the white deviant cities.

The level of per capita expenditures on health and hospitals was the major single variable in this regression. It alone accounts for 11 percent of the possible variance. The average payment per family under the program of Aid to Families with Dependent Children (AFDC) contributed 8 percent to our understanding. The level of per capita revenue and the rate of AFDC add respectively 4 and 2 percent.

Although these variables appear to be interrelated on the surface,

---

[5]See Appendix A for a complete discussion of our second analysis stage, especially pages 82-85.

Table 2-5
Independent Components of White Dropout Residual Regression, Secondary
Variables Only, for Deviant Cities and Their Contributions to Total Pre-
dicted Variance

Independent Components of Regression	Contributions		
	Beta	Zero Order r	Percent of Relative Contribution to Total Predicted Variance[a]
45.[b] Expenditures on Health and Hospitals	0.3253	.35	11%
50. Average Payment Per Family of AFDC	−0.3531	−.22	8
46. Revenue	0.1690	.23	4
49. Rate of AFDC	−0.1522	−.13	2
	R = .50		25%

[a]See Table 2-1, page 17.
[b]See Table 2-1.
[c]Significant at .05 level.

this is not entirely true, as Table 2-6 demonstrates. High expenditures on health and hospitals do not necessitate high payments per
family of AFDC, or a high rate of AFDC. In fact, there is a slight
negative relationship between the incidence of families with dependent children and the expenditures on the other two variables. Per
capita revenue correlates positively with all of the other variables,
but this correlation is only of a moderate nature. Richer cities have
a tendency to spend more on health and welfare, but this is not always,
or necessarily, true.

Deviant cities with high revenues and high per capita expenditures
on health and hospitals, and with low rates and payments per family
of AFDC, are more often "above" cities as compared to other deviant
communities. Deviant cities with the reverse pattern comparatively
tend to appear as "below" communities.

Table 2-6
Correlation Matrix of Secondary Variables Included in White
Dropout Residual Regression for Deviant Cities

Variables	45	50	49
50	23		
49	−04	−02	
46	60	31	16

Discussion

WHEN the results of the original multiple regression are kept in
mind, these findings take on additional meaning. We found that cities
which are more disadvantaged economically exhibit higher white
dropout rates. Public expenditures on health and hospitals do not
reduce economically depressed conditions; they merely provide basic
and necessary services for a population which might be unable to pro-

Table 2-7
Independent Components of White Dropout Residual Regression, Primary and
Secondary Variables, for Deviant Cities and Their Contributions to Total Pre-
dicted Variance

Independent Components of Regression	Beta	Contributions	
		Zero Order r	Percent of Relative Contribution to Total Predicted Variance[a]
50.[b] Average Payment Per Family of AFDC	−0.8390	−.22	18%
22. White Adult Illiteracy Rate	0.6966	.20	14
45. Expenditures on Health and Hospitals	0.3859	.35	14
2. Population Per Square Mile	0.5981	.18	11
32. Percent of White Male Operatives	0.9690	.10	10
14. Percent of White Income Under $1,000	0.5083	.15	8
43. Per Pupil Expenditures	−0.4102	−.10	4
17. Percent of White Income $10,000 or More	0.7557	−.01	−1[c]
41. Percent Males 35-44 Not in Labor Force	−0.3245	.09	−3[c]
4. Percent Increase in Population, 1950-1960	0.2765	−.14	−4[c]
26. Percent in White Collar Occupations	0.8420	−.12	−10[c]
		R = .78[d]	61%

[a]See Table 2-1, page 17.
[b]See Table 2-1.
[c]See Table 2-1.
[d]Significant at the .01 level.

Table 2-8
Correlation Matrix of Major, Primary and Secondary Variables
Included in White Dropout Regression for Deviant Cities

Variables	50	22	45	2
22	27			
45	23	15		
2	45	29	52	
32	41	66	−00	33

vide these services for itself. Payments per family for AFDC, on the
other hand, help to alleviate depressed conditions by providing *additional* (Federal) income for deprived families — the net effect being
greater when the payments are higher. In the same way, the larger
the number of families receiving some assistance, the larger are the
chances of reducing abject poverty to some degree and, therefore, the
lower the white dropout rate. The importance of the rate of AFDC and
the per capita revenue of the city, in explaining the residual variance,
however, is minimal, as can be seen when the primary variables are
included in the regression.

When both the original and the secondary variables are used to explain deviance on the white dropout rate, per capita revenue and the
rate of AFDC no longer appear as large contributors to total predicted variance. The new multiple R is .78, and we are now able to
explain an additional 31 percent of the residual variance or a total of
61 percent.

Average payment per family for AFDC now becomes the prime contributor, accounting for 18 percent of the possible variance. Public
expenditures on health and hospitals take on secondary importance,
contributing 14 percent. Together, they now account for slightly more
than half of the explained variance (32%) among white deviant cities.

The findings support the thesis advanced in one discussion of the
secondary variables alone: *Deviant communities with relatively more
favorable social and economic conditions — low levels of illiteracy,
population density, male operatives, and expenditures on health and
hospitals — and high average payments per family for AFDC which
help to alleviate the conditions of poverty, are more likely to have
lower white dropout rates than expected, when compared to other deviant cities.* Communities with the opposite social and economic conditions, and low average AFDC payments, are more likely to be deviant in a negative direction, or "above" the expected dropout rate.

Nonwhite Deviant Case Analysis

THE multiple correlation between the nonwhite residual and selected
secondary variables was R = .58. These variables, therefore, accounted

Table 2-9
Independent Components of Nonwhite Residual Regression, Secondary Varia-
bles Only, for Deviant Cities and Their Contributions to Total Predicted
Variance

Independent Components of Regression	Contributions		
	Beta	Zero Order r	Percent of Relative Contribution to Total Predicted Variance[a]
43.[b] Per Pupil Expenditures	0.4517	.47	21%
50. Average Payment Per Family of AFDC	0.3099	.37	11
44. Expenditures on Parks and Recreation	−0.1754	−.01	0
		R = .58[c]	32%

[a]See Table 2-1, page 17.
[b]See Table 2-1.
[c]Significant at the .01 level.

Table 2-10
Correlation Matrix of Secondary Variables
Included in Nonwhite Dropout Residual
Regression for Deviant Cities

Variables	43	50
50	21	
44	24	18

for 32 percent of the possible variance among the nonwhite deviant
cities.

As we can see, all of the explained variance was accounted for by
two variables — per pupil expenditures (21%) and the average payment
per family of AFDC (11%). The latter variable thus contributes to understanding of both the white and nonwhite residual variance.

The importance of these variables was not changed when we included

Table 2-11

Independent Components of Nonwhite Dropout Residual Regression, Primary and Secondary Variables, for Deviant Cities and Their Contributions to Total Predicted Variance

Independent Components of Regression	Contributions		
	Beta	Zero Order r	Percent of Relative Contribution to Total Predicted Variance[a]
43.[b] Per Pupil Expenditures	0.8505	.47	40%
50. Average Payment of AFDC	0.6979	.37	26
45. Expenditures on Health and Hospitals	0.7097	.20	14
41. Percent of Males 35-44 Not in Labor Force	−0.2939	−.35	10
13. Percent Population Between 5-18 Years	1.0056	.05	5
39. Percent Nonwhite Female Private Household Workers	−0.1450	−.27	4
40. Sex Ratio	−0.5409	−.04	2
37. Percent Nonwhite Male Service Workers	−0.2669	−.05	1
26. Percent in White Collar Occupations	0.2996	.03	1
10. Fertility Ratio	−0.5123	.00	−0
2. Population Per Square Mile	−0.5075	.03	−1[c]
35. Percent Nonwhite Male Professionals	−0.3406	.10	−3[c]
19. Percent Nonwhite Income Between $1,000-$1,999	0.2800	−.20	−6[c]
	R = .97[d]		93%

[a]See Table 2-1, page 17.
[b]See Table 2-1.
[c]See Table 2-1.
[d]Significant at .01 level.

Table 2-12
Correlation Matrix of Major Primary and Secondary Variables
Included in Nonwhite Dropout Residual Regression for Deviant
Cities

Variables	43	50	45
50	21		
45	−01	15	
41	−22	−17	31

the primary variables; their contributions were increased. When the original social and economic variables are reintroduced, we obtain a new multiple R of .97. We thus explain an additional 61 percent of the residual variance, or a total of 93 percent. It is interesting to note that here we were able to explain one-third more of the variance on the nonwhite residual than the white. Furthermore, while the additions of the primary variables in the white residual resulted in the inclusion of three of these as major contributors to total predicted variance, the same pattern did not obtain on the nonwhite residual regression.[6]

The results of the nonwhite residual regression are more difficult to explain than those of the white residual. Deviant cities with high levels of per pupil, health, and welfare expenditures and low percentages of males not in the labor force are more apt to have higher nonwhite dropout rates than expected. Cities exhibiting the opposite patterns are more likely to be deviant in a positive direction and thus considered "below" expected.

The three major contributors in this regression have a positive relationship to the residual. The influence of average payments per family for AFDC is, therefore, in an opposite direction here than on the white residual.

Two factors might be contributing to this pattern. First, the secondary variables are indicators of public expenditures for the city as a whole. We were not able to secure separate figures, for example, on the average payments per family for AFDC for the white and nonwhite population. Therefore, it is very possible that the effects of these

---

[6]As reference to Table 2-11 shows, 80 percent of the possible variance, or 86 percent of the explained variance, is accounted for by the secondary variables of per pupil, welfare, and health expenditures. Only 10 percent stems from one primary variable—the percentage of males 35 to 44 not in the labor force. In contrast, the secondary variables on the white residual accounted for 32 percent of the possible variance or only 53 percent of the explained variance.

expenditures are differently received among whites and nonwhites, with the white population receiving more of the benefits.

Secondly, if the results of the original nonwhite dropout regression are kept in mind, the findings here become more understandable. As was indicated in the discussion of the white residual, payments of AFDC help to alleviate depressed conditions by providing additional income. Although this is true, the fact remains that welfare assistance is necessary. The higher the payments, the more visible they become, and conversely, the less incentive there is to remain in school as chances for betterment through education are perceived as slight. In the same sense, the level of per pupil expenditures, as such, does not have as direct an effect on the nonwhite population as the white. When education is used as a means to an end, it becomes useful only when the end seems obtainable.

CONCLUSION

IN summary, we were more successful in explaining the variance on the nonwhite residual than the white. Unlike the original regressions, there was overlapping on the factors accounting for the deviant status of the cities. Average payments per family for AFDC and expenditures on health and hospitals are major contributors to the explanation of the variance on both regressions. Per pupil expenditures was the other major contributor on the nonwhite residual, while the white illiteracy rate, population per square mile, and the percent of white operatives provided additional understanding of the deviance on the white dropout rate.

In conclusion, we have shown that differences in levels of high school dropouts are functions of social and economic differences across the largest cities in the United States, white and nonwhite rates having varying correlates. In addition, we have demonstrated that departures of cities from expected levels of high school withdrawal, given their social and economic conditions, are related in large part to differences in per capita welfare, health, and educational program expenditures. These factors exert differing influences on white and nonwhite withdrawal. The significance of the results in both of these spheres for policy and program decisions will be discussed after the analysis of the second educational barrier —adult functional illiteracy.

CHAPTER 3

EXPLAINING ADULT FUNCTIONAL ILLITERACY

THE traditional index of adult functional illiteracy—adults reporting less than five years of elementary schooling in the decennial census—was used for specification of our second major dependent variable. The methodological design of this part of the study was the same as that employed in the analysis of the white and nonwhite dropout rates, and was based on the same 131 large cities in the United States. In this chapter we will discuss the social and economic correlates of adult functional illiteracy across these 131 cities, and the features of those communities which reveal much higher or lower rates than expected.

WHITE ILLITERACY

THE multiple correlation between the white adult illiteracy[1] rate and selected social and economic characteristics of the cities was R = .84. These social and economic variables have, therefore, accounted for 70 percent of the possible variance.

As Table 3-1 demonstrates, the principal factors in this equation, and their relative contributions to total predicted variance are: percent of white in-migration (27%), percent of the labor force in white

---

[1]"Functional illiteracy" and "illiteracy" will be used synonymously throughout the book.

Table 3-1

Independent Components of White Adult Functional Illiteracy Regression and Their Contributions to Total Predicted Variance

Independent Components of Regression		Contributions		
		Beta	Zero Order r	Percent of Relative Contribution to Total Predicted Variance[a]
29.[b]	Percent White In-Migration	−0.4677	−.57	27%
26.	Percent in White Collar Occupations	−0.4304	−.59	25
14.	Percent White Income Under $1,000	0.3097	.42	13
33.	Percent White Male Service Workers	0.2668	.33	9
10.	Fertility Ratio	−0.4620	−.11	5
34.	Percent White Male Operatives	0.1122	.35	4
28.	Percent Occupied Units with 1.01+ Per Room	0.2588	.14	4
53.	Median Rent	−0.0643	−.28	2
11.	Nonworker Ratio	0.0763	.03	0
41.	Percent Males 35-44 Not in Labor Force	−0.0864	.07	−1[c]
12.	Percent Population Under 5 Years	0.2138	−.10	−2[c]
40.	Sex Ratio	0.1948	−.15	−3[c]
4.	Percent Increase in Population 1950-1960	0.0972	−.43	−4[c]
31.	Percent White Male Professionals	0.1632	−.53	−9[c]
			R = .84[d]	70%

[a]See Table 2-1, page 17.
[b]See Table 2-1.
[c]See Table 2-1.
[d]Significant at .01 level.

Table 3-2
Correlation Matrix of Major Variables Included in White
Adult Functional Illiteracy Regression

Variables	29	26	14
26	43		
14	01	−28	
33	−31	−05	12

collar occupations (25%), percent of white families with incomes under $1,000 (13%), and the percent of white male service workers (9%).

Knowledge of the level of white in-migration and white collar workers in a city provide approximately equal understanding of the white
illiteracy rate. However, either one contributes twice as much knowledge as that supplied by the percent of low income families and three
times as much as is gained from the level of white male service
workers.

In addition to differing in their relative contributions to total predicted variance, these four variables have different relationships to
illiteracy. Two have a positive relation to the white illiteracy rate,
while two are negatively associated. Cities having low levels of white
in-migration and white collar workers and high percentages of low income families and male service workers, compared to other cities,
have high levels of white adult illiteracy. Communities in which the
reverse pattern obtains have a comparatively low white illiteracy
rate.[2]

As we would expect from the importance of the white illiteracy
rate as a correlate of premature withdrawal from high school, there
is considerable overlapping of the social and economic conditions of
communities having high illiteracy and dropout rates. The level of
white collar workers and low income families appear as important
correlates in both regressions. Once again we see the strong relationship between poverty and low educational attainment. Poor communities have less literate adult populations.

---

[2]After the completion of the study, we realized that the failure to con-
sider percent foreign born as an independent variable on the white adult
illiteracy regression might be a serious omission. We, therefore, selected
a random sample of 25 cities and computed a Pearsonian r between these
two variables. The resulting r = .29 was not significant at the .05 level and
was of lower magnitude than the zero order r's of the principal factors in
the regression equation. We thus concluded that the omission of this variable
would not significantly alter the obtained results.

The reader must be cautioned not to infer a causal relationship where poor occupational and income achievement leads to illiteracy, however. We are dealing here with the adult population who were 25 years of age or older in 1960, using the social and economic conditions of cities at this time as independent variables. The educational level of these adults was established in the past, thus present conditions do not have a direct effect.

Yet, those cities which are comparatively disadvantaged and static have a larger adult illiterate population than cities with a different occupational, income, and in-migration mix.

NONWHITE ILLITERACY

THE results of the nonwhite adult illiteracy regression are on the whole similar to those of the white regression. Here, we obtained a multiple correlation of R = .91. This accounts for 82 percent of the possible variance on the nonwhite illiteracy rate — more than on any of the other dependent variables.

The principal components of this equation and their relative contribution to the total predicted variance are: percent of nonwhite male laborers (32%), percent of nonwhite family income between $1,000-$1,999 (10%), percent of nonwhite female private household workers (9%), percent of the nonwhite population in 1950 (8%), percent of nonwhite family income under $1,000 (8%) percent of nonwhite in-migration (6%), and finally the percent of nonwhite male operatives (6%).[3]

As in the dropout regressions, comparative statements can be made concerning the respective importance of factors accounting for *both* white and nonwhite illiteracy. The level of in-migration is an important contributor to both regressions, but its influence in the white regression is greater than in the nonwhite. In the former, knowledge of the white in-migration rate added 27% to total possible

---

[3]There was a much wider variation in the relative contributions of the variables in the nonwhite illiteracy regression than there was on the white regression. In the latter, the first two variables had approximately the same relative contribution to total predicted variance (27 and 25%), and they provided only 3 times as much as the last factor, which added 9%. In the nonwhite regression, the relative contribution of the first variable—percent of nonwhite male laborers—is higher than either major contributor on the white regression (32%), and provides three times as much understanding as the second factor and more than five times as much as the last two factors. Therefore, the difference in contribution of the first two variables on the nonwhite regression is equal to the total spread on the whole white illiteracy regression.

Table 3-3

Independent Components of Nonwhite Adult Functional Illiteracy Regression and Their Contributions to Total Predicted Variance

Independent Components of Regression		Beta	Contributions	
			Zero Order r	Percent of Relative Contribution to Total Predicted Variance[a]
38.[b]	Percent Nonwhite Male Laborers	0.4242	.76	32%
19.	Percent Nonwhite Income Between $1,000–$1,999	0.1474	.69	10
30.	Percent Nonwhite Female Private Household Workers	0.1345	.66	9
6.	Percent Nonwhite, 1950	0.1199	.70	8
18.	Percent Nonwhite Income Under $1,000	0.1108	.68	8
30.	Percent Nonwhite In-Migration	−0.1824	−.34	6
36.	Percent Nonwhite Male Operatives	0.1845	.31	6
13.	Percent Population Between 5–18 Years	0.1346	.26	4
41.	Percent Males 35–44 Not in Labor Force	0.1114	.30	3
26.	Percent in White Collar Occupations	−0.0946	−.32	3
7.	Percent Increase in Nonwhite population 1950–1960	−0.1520	−.11	2
10.	Fertility Ratio	−0.1729	.03	−1[c]
2.	Population Per Square Mile	0.0586	−.15	−1[c]
21.	Percent Nonwhite Income $10,000 or More	0.1145	−.30	−3[c]
9.	Percent Nonwhite Non-Negro 1960	0.0944	−.41	−4[c]
			R = .91[d]	82%

[a]See Table 2-1, page 17.
[b]See Table 2-1.
[c]See Table 2-1.
[d]Significant at .01 level.

Table 3-4
Correlation Matrix of Major Variables Included in Nonwhite Adult
Functional Illiteracy Regression

Variables	38	19	39	6	18	30
19	56					
39	62	71				
6	56	57	52			
18	54	77	57	49		
30	−11	−23	−14	−34	−27	
36	24	07	06	28	27	02

predicted variance, or 38% of the explained variance. The level of
nonwhite in-migration contributes 6% to the nonwhite regression, or
8% of the explained variance. Therefore, the level of in-migration
has a negative relationship to both the white and nonwhite illiteracy
rates, yet the magnitude of the relationship is much stronger on the
white regression.

Similarly, the percentages of impoverished white and nonwhite
families (those with income of less than $1,000) are important con-
tributors to total predicted variance on *both* regressions. White family income under $1,000 adds 13% to the total possible predicted vari-
ance on the white regression, or 19% of the explained variance. The
respective figures for nonwhite income under $1,000 are 8% and 9%.
Here again, very low income achievement provides more understanding of the white illiteracy rate than the nonwhite. However, if we include the percent of nonwhite families with income between $1,000 -
$1,999, then the level of nonwhite low income families contributes
18% to total predicted variance or 21% of the explained variance, and
the relative contribution of low income achievement becomes comparable on both regressions.

The occupational variables do not refer to the same populations.
Therefore, similar comparable statements have little utility. However, as the reader can see, the relationship between low occupational
achievement and illiteracy is strong on both the white and nonwhite
regressions.

As we indicated above, the results of the nonwhite illiteracy regression are very similar to those of the white. Once again we see
the relationship between poverty and low educational achievement:
*Communities having high percentages of white male laborers and op-
eratives, female private household workers, low income families and
nonwhites in 1950 and a low nonwhite in-migration rate, compared to
other cities, have high nonwhite adult illiteracy rates.* Communities

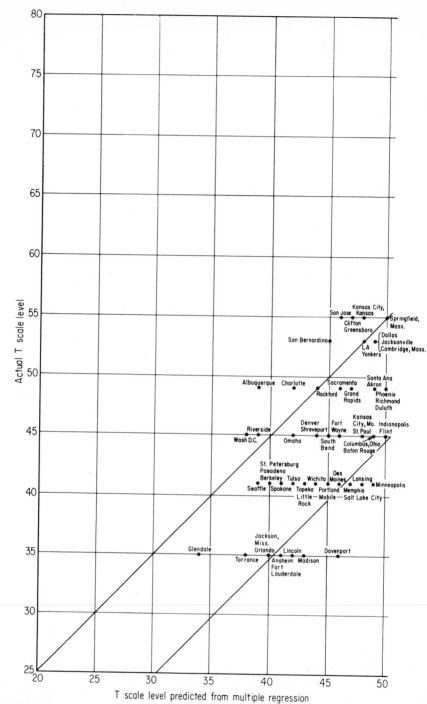

Figure 3-1
GRAPH OF T SCALE LEVEL OF WHITE ADULT FUNCTIONAL ILLIT-
ERACY FOR 131 CITIES, BY T SCALE LEVEL PREDICTED FROM
MULTIPLE REGRESSION.*

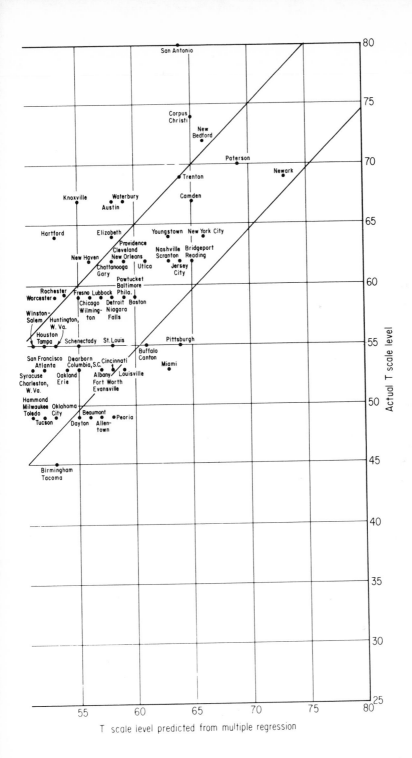

*From 1960 United States census data. Diagonal lines are error bands.

43

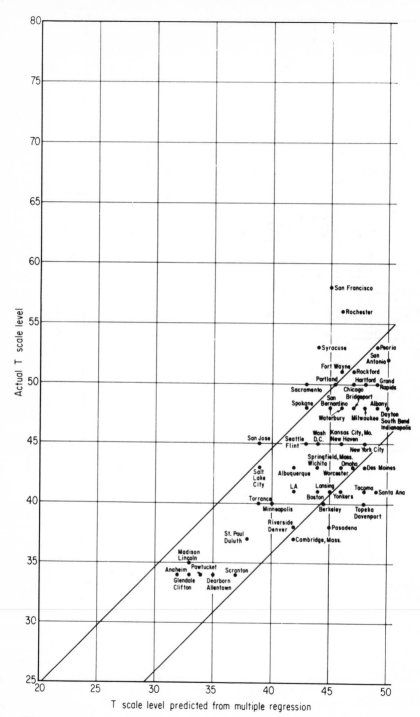

Figure 3-2
GRAPH OF T SCALE LEVEL OF NONWHITE ADULT FUNCTIONAL
ILLITERACY FOR 131 CITIES, BY T SCALE LEVEL PREDICTED
FROM MULTIPLE REGRESSION.*

44

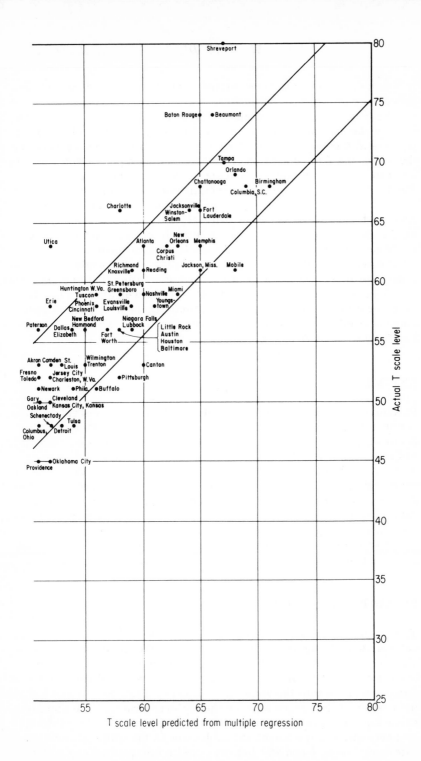

*From 1960 United States census data. Diagonal lines are error bands.

45

in which the reverse pattern obtains would have a comparatively low percentage of nonwhite illiterates.

The only new component appearing as a major contributor is the level of the nonwhite population in 1950. Given a relatively disadvantaged, static community, the larger the population a decade earlier, the more likely the conditions connected with a high nonwhite illiteracy rate will be maintained, and subsequently, the higher the rate. The high positive zero order correlations between this variable and most other factors in the regression add support to this supposition. Also, in these cities, the adult illiteracy rate in 1960 is likely to be higher as many of the young people in 1950 turn 25 and, therefore, would be considered as part of the *adult* illiterate population.

The results of this regression add support to the analysis and discussion of the nonwhite dropout regression. Cities that are relatively disadvantaged and static communities, offer fewer avenues for advancement or security through education. Therefore, such impoverished communities have a higher percentage of nonwhite dropouts as well as higher adult illiteracy rates.

RESUME

IN summary, both white and nonwhite adult illiteracy correlate with low in-migration and high levels of low income and occupational achievement. In addition, the level of the nonwhite population in 1950 had importance for the understanding of the nonwhite illiteracy rate. These factors account for 70 percent of the variance of the white illiteracy rate and 82 percent of the variance on the nonwhite regression. Here we were more successful in identifying the factors connected with nonwhite adult illiteracy. As in the analysis of the dropout rates, factors such as population density, unemployment and median rent added little or nothing to our understanding of low adult educational achievement when the above factors were taken into account.

DEVIANT CASE ANALYSIS

THE second stage of this analysis was exactly the same as the dropout analysis. Using the above correlated social and economic variables, white and nonwhite illiteracy rates were predicted for each of the 131 cities. By comparing the actual and predicted rates, we classified the cities into the same three groups. Figures 3-1 and 3-2 show the results of this procedure for the illiteracy rates. The standard error for the white illiteracy rate is 5.38; for the nonwhite it is 4.41.

Forty cities were classified as deviant on the white illiteracy rate — 20 "above" and 20 "below" — while thirty-two were so labeled on the nonwhite rate — 15 "above" and 17 "below." Nine cities were deviant on both variables: Pittsburgh, Buffalo, Davenport, Canton, Tacoma, Charlotte, San Jose, Rochester, and Beaumont. All of these cities, with the exception of Beaumont, are deviant in the same direction on both rates — the first five "below" and the next three "above." Beaumont is "below" on the white and "above" on the nonwhite illiteracy rate.

In summary, only one city — Rochester — was classified as deviant on all four dependent variables. Five communities were labeled deviant on three of the variables, thirty-three on two, fifty-three on only one, and thirty-nine were consistently classified as non-deviant.[4]

White Deviant Case Analysis

THE multiple correlation between the white residual and selected secondary variables was R = .46. These indicators thus accounted for 21 percent of the variance among deviant cities on white illiteracy levels.

Table 3-5
Independent Components of White Adult Functional Illiteracy Residual Regression, Secondary Variables Only, for Deviant Cities, and Their Contributions to Total Predicted Variance

Independent Components of Regression	Contributions		
	Beta	Zero Order r	Percent of Relative Contribution to Total Predicted Variance[a]
45.[b] Expenditures on Health and Hospitals	0.3116	.38	12%
49. Rate of AFDC	0.2667	.25	7
44. Expenditures on Parks and Recreation	−0.1862	−.12	2
		R = .46[c]	21%

[a]See Table 2-1, page 17.
[b]See Table 2-1.
[c]Significant at .05 level.

---

[4]For a detailed listing of the deviant vs. non-deviant status of each city on all four variables, see Table B-6 in Appendix B.

Table 3-6
Correlation Matrix of Secondary Variables Included in White Adult Functional Illiteracy Regression for Deviant Cities

Variables	45	49
49	18	
44	−11	37

Per capita expenditures on health and hospitals is the major variable on this regression, accounting for 12 percent of the possible variance. The rate of AFDC contributes 7 percent, while per capita expenditures on parks and recreation adds 2 percent. Thus, deviant cities with high expenditures on health and hospitals, and rates of AFDC,
and low expenditures on parks and recreation are more likely to have
higher white illiteracy rates compared to other deviant communities.
Cities with the reverse pattern are more likely to be classified as
"below."

The addition of the primary variables to the equation had the chief
effect of increasing the importance of the first two variables. It also
eliminated the influence of per capita expenditures on parks and recreation as a contributor.

Here, the new multiple R = .73 enabled us to explain an additional
27 percent of the residual variance, or a total of 53 percent. Per
capita expenditures on health and hospitals now account for 27 rather
than 12 percent of the variance, while the rate of AFDC contributes
14 instead of 7 percent.

When the results of the original illiteracy regression are kept in
mind, these results take on additional meaning. Cities with rather depressed conditions — low income and occupational achievement, and
low in-migration rates — have a higher number of white adult illiterates. Given these conditions, high per capita expenditures on health
and hospitals might indicate the need for the city to provide basic and
necessary services for a large segment of the population unable to
meet these needs privately. Likewise, a high incidence of children
receiving aid under AFDC would indicate a more dependent population,
one likely to have no private means of securing support or assistance.
Therefore, these communities would be more disadvantaged than expected and, hence, would have more white adult illiterates than expected.[5]

---

[5]This interpretation assumes a process over time, while our data are
rather static. Therefore, this interpretation is quite speculative.

Table 3-7
Independent Components of White Adult Functional Illiteracy Residual Regression, Primary and Secondary Variables, for Deviant Cities and Their Contributions to Total Predicted Variance

Independent Components of Regression	Beta	Zero Order r	Percent of Relative Contribution to Total Predicted Variance[a]
		Contributions	
45.[b] Expenditures on Health and Hospitals	0.7212	.38	27%
49. Rate of AFDC	0.5650	.25	14
4. Percent Increase in Population 1950-1960	0.6226	.06	4
2. Population Per Square Mile	−0.3239	−.11	4
10. Fertility Ratio	0.1977	.14	3
44. Expenditures on Parks and Recreation	−0.1916	−.12	2
29. Percent White In-Migration	−0.6941	−.02	1
17. Percent White Income $10,000+	−0.2789	−.05	1
24. Percent White Unemployment	0.3404	.04	1
14. Percent White Income Under $1,000	0.2577	.05	1
3. Total Population, 1960	−0.2245	−.03	1
41. Percent Males 35-44 Not in Labor Force	0.1497	−.02	−0[c]
11. Nonworker Ratio	−0.3584	.05	−2[c]
53. Median Rent	0.5095	−.08	−4[c]
		R = .73[d]	53%

[a]See Table 2-1, page 17.
[b]See Table 2-1.
[c]See Table 2-1.
[d]Significant at .01 level.

Table 3-8
Correlation Matrix of Major Primary and Secondary Variables
Included in White Adult Functional Illiteracy Residual Regression
for Deviant Cities

Variables	45	49	4
49	18		
4	− 24	− 02	
2	11	− 05	− 58

The influence of population increase and population density are
less discernible. Given a low white in-migration rate, a high rate of
population increase could result from a high birth rate, with the subsequent increase of the very young population. The zero order r's
between population increase and the population under five (r = .56)
and the fertility ratio (r = .49) seem to substantiate this. As was indicated in the analysis of the white dropout rate, the presence of a
large number of young children compounds conditions of poverty; it
presents additional pressures for support and subsistence in an already disadvantaged community. Therefore, the effect of age structure would be similar to that of per capita expenditures on health and
hospitals and the rate of AFDC. High levels of all of these variables
are associated with more depressed conditions.

Although high population density in a relatively disadvantaged community usually has the effects of accentuating the conditions of poverty, this variable has a negative relation to the white residual. Given
the other factors in the regression, low population density would be
associated with higher levels of white adult illiterates than expected.
The negative zero order r's between density and population increase
(r = -.58), percent of the population under five years of age (r = -.50),
and the fertility ratio (r = -.49), seem to indicate that a *natural* increase in the population is inversely associated with the density of
the community. This may be due to the lower in-migration and higher
out-migration rates which cancel the effects of a high birth rate.

Given this fact and the positive association between density and
total population (r = .38), however, the effects of this variable become
understandable: Cities with high numbers of adult illiterates may at-
tract a lower proportion of in-migrants from other states. The negative zero order r's between the level of in-migration, low income,
and low occupational attainment, suggests that this type of static population is in a relatively *less* advantageous state. Given low rates of
in-migration and the positive association between density and total

population, it is likely that "above" cities comparatively would be smaller, less settled communities. Perhaps, too, the population living in these cities are apt to be more socially and economically disadvantaged when the *effects* of in-and-out-migration are considered. The city is likely to be less viable, have higher dependency and birth rates and more white adult illiterates than expected.

Thus, deviant cities with high per capita expenditures on health and hospitals, dependency rates, and population increase (attributed mainly to the birth rate) and low population density tend to be more socially and economically depressed communities and are likely to have higher levels of white adult illiteracy. Cities with more favorable conditions are likely to have lower rates than expected and are classified as "below."

NONWHITE DEVIANT CASE ANALYSIS

THE multiple correlation between the nonwhite residual and the secondary variables only was not significant. When both the primary and secondary variables were used to explain the deviance on the nonwhite illiteracy rate, however, we obtained a multiple R = .91, and we were able to explain 83 percent of the possible variance among the nonwhite deviant cities.

The prime contributors here, in contrast to the white data, are not city government expenditures (they take a secondary importance, accounting together for 23 percent of the variance), but the social and economic conditions of the deviant cities. The major correlates are now the level of nonwhite female dependency and the nonworker ratio, which account for 42 percent of the explained variance. The other principal correlates and their relative contribution to the total predicted variance are: per pupil expenditures (14%), average payment per family for AFDC (9%), percent of the population under 5 (7%), median rent (7%), and the sex ratio (4%).

Therefore, cities with *high* levels of nonwhite dependent females, nonworkers, median rent, and more males than females, and cities with *low* levels of per pupil expenditures, average payments of AFDC and children under 5, are more often "below" cities as compared to other deviant communities. Cities exhibiting the opposite patterns are more apt to have *higher* nonwhite illiteracy rates than expected.

Upon first inspection, the results of this regression seem quite surprising. The prime contributor to total predicted variance—*the percent of nonwhite female dependency*—has a negative relation to the dependent variable! This seems to contradict the notion of a strong positive relationship between welfare dependency and illiteracy. (Our variable is not a pure indicator of nonwhite female dependency but is a ratio of the number of females aged 14-65, with children

Table 3-9

Independent Components of Nonwhite Adult Functional Illiteracy Residual
Regression, Primary and Secondary Variables, for Deviant Cities and Their
Contributions to Total Predicted Variance

Independent Components of Regression	Beta	Zero Order r	Percent of Relative Contribution to Total Predicted Variance[a]
		Contributions	
42.[b] Percent Nonwhite Female Dependency	−1.0011	−.20	20%
11. Nonworker Ratio	−1.1303	−.13	15
43. Per Pupil Expenditures	0.6202	.23	14
50. Average Payment Per Family for AFDC	0.7283	.12	9
12. Percent Population Under 5 Years	1.6831	.04	7
53. Median Rent	−0.8651	−.08	7
40. Sex Ratio	−0.3524	−.11	4
21. Percent Nonwhite Income, $10,000 or More	−0.7562	−.03	2
28. Percent Occupied Units with 1.01+ Per Room	−0.7050	−.03	2
5. Percent Nonwhite in 1960	0.1090	.17	2
45. Expenditures on Health and Hospitals	0.1566	.09	1
		R = .91[c]	83%

[a]See Table 2-1, page 17.
[b]See Table 2-1.
[c]Significant at .01 level.

Table 3-10

Correlation Matrix Primary and Secondary Variables Included in Nonwhite
Illiteracy Residual Regression for Deviant Cities

Variables	42	11	43	50	12	53
11	−11					
43	09	−42				
50	25	−42	75			
12	−17	71	−65	−50		
53	−23	−42	53	55	−23	
40	−12	24	−28	06	56	11

under 6 whose husbands are not present, to the number of females aged 14-65, not in the labor force, school or an institution.) However, the zero order r's for the 131 cities in our sample show positive correlation between this variable and the percent of nonwhite unemployment ($r = .51$), nonwhite operatives ($r = .35$), white service workers ($r = .31$), and negative correlations with the percent of population increase ($r = -.38$) and population living in structures built in 1950 or later ($r = -.40$). In view of these correlations, our variable seems to be a good approximation of nonwhite female dependency and, therefore, its relationship to the illiteracy residual is not discernible at once.

When *all* of the components of this equation and the results of the first nonwhite regression are considered, however, the above pattern takes on meaning. Nonwhite adult illiteracy correlated highly with conditions indicative of extreme poverty: high percentages of low income families, male laborers and operatives, female private household workers, and a low percentage of nonwhite in-migration. Therefore, disadvantaged, static communities tend to exhibit high nonwhite illiteracy rates.

Under these conditions, a nonwhite female with a young child and no husband would likely have no means of securing support or assistance other than welfare payments. The presumed positive association between dependency and illiteracy is based on just this dependent population.

Three variables, besides nonwhite female dependency, had a negative relation to the residual. The nonworker ratio, as our discussion of the nonwhite dropout rate showed, is probably an indicator of the number of children in school and the number of housewives and mothers not in the labor force. The sex ratio refers to the population aged 35-44, a higher ratio indicating a higher proportion of males of this age, and the higher proportion of possible wage earners, husbands, fathers and providers. Therefore, high levels of these two variables and median rent would generally be more prevalent in cities that were relatively "better off," or cities that had a smaller young population which subsequently posed fewer problems of support, and in cities where the average payment per family for AFDC was lower because support was not as widely needed.

Given these conditions, a high percentage of females with young children and no husbands would have different implications than in an impoverished community. Although a small part of the poorer population is apt to be on welfare, it is likely that the large majority will not be. These females are probably more likely to be widows, with some money to provide for themselves and their children. Furthermore, with favorable conditions existing in the community, these women probably exist as dependents of kin or friends, without entering the labor force or receiving welfare assistance.

These women would not "have" to enter the labor force, thus there would be more job opportunities for both the male sector and those females that do have to support themselves and their children, especially in the usual female white-collar positions. The occupational and income mix of the community is likely to be more favorable than expected and the nonwhite adult illiteracy rates are also apt to be lower, leading to the classification of these cities as "below."

In summary, the factors related to the nonwhite residual differ from those which were major contributors in the white residual regression. However, the import of both is similar: Deviant cities with more favorable social and economic conditions have lower adult illiteracy rates than expected, compared to other communities, while those that are more disadvantaged are more likely to be classified as "above."

CHAPTER 4

INTERPRETATIONS

FINDINGS REVIEWED

OUR empirical analysis supports consistently our main hypotheses: variations in dropout rates and levels of adult illiteracy across 131 of the largest American cities are functions of differences in levels of poverty, occupational mix, economic opportunity and social mobility, among the cities. Also, we found, as we hypothesized, that how cities expend their public funds for health, welfare, and education is indeed associated with their citizens' educational characteristics. But in this instance we were only generally correct, as we shall indicate below.

Our analysis supports our contention that withdrawing from high school before graduation is *not* an individual event to be diagnosed, prevented, or otherwise treated individually. There are significant psychological processes involved in dropping out, to be sure, but these are so structured that, in the aggregate, they occur only under predictable community conditions.

Dearborn, Michigan, for example, has a white dropout rate half that of most cities, and a third of the rate for Nashville, Tennessee, as of 1960. This difference is not randomly distributed. Rather, white youths withdraw from high school three times more frequently in Nashville than in Dearborn because the *context* of economic and social opportunities in Dearborn is that much more favorable to youths.

The term context refers here to the fact that big cities with expanding white collar job markets also tend to be cities with more favorable

Table 4-1
Mean Dropout and Adult Illiteracy Rates by Ethnicity and Region

Region	Percent Dropout		Percent Adult Illiteracy		N
	White	Nonwhite	White	Nonwhite	
New England–Middle Atlantic	18.2	30.8	8.6	14.0[a]	33
East and West North Central	17.0	25.2	5.0	12.0[b]	36
South	18.9	27.2	6.4	21.7	39
Mountain and Pacific	13.8	20.0	4.3	11.4[c]	23

[a]Mean is based on an N of 29 cities. Four cities with less than 1% non-white were eliminated. See discussion in Appendix A, p. 80.

[b]Mean is based on an N of 35 cities. See discussion in Appendix A.

[c]Mean is based on an N of 21 cities. See discussion in Appendix A.

income levels, housing, and employment security. Such cities as Nashville, St. Louis, Louisville, Cincinnati, and Jacksonville, offered fewer work opportunities and carried relatively larger numbers of impoverished families than did such cities as Dearborn, Portland, Berkeley, and Pasadena, in 1960. We have deliberately chosen cities to contrast that are situated in different cultural *regions* of the United States. In fact, repeated analysis revealed that *region is not correlated* with either dropout rate or adult illiteracy after the social and economic differences of the various cities have been considered.

We are *not* saying that regional differences in levels of high school withdrawal and adult illiteracy do not obtain. As Table 4-1 shows, there is variation on the four dependent variables across regions. The cities located in the Mountain-Pacific states tend to have the *lowest* mean rates. Southern communities, on the other hand, show disproportionally higher nonwhite adult illiteracy rates and higher white dropout rates. Although these differences exist for the total sample, they do not obtain for those cities that deviated from expectancy on any one dependent variable. [1] In other words, cities with much higher or lower dropout or adult illiteracy rates than expected, given their social and economic conditions, are not more often located in one region compared to another. Therefore, once the social and economic characteristics of the various cultural regions have been taken into account, region is randomly associated with high school withdrawal or adult illiteracy.

---

[1]The obtained Gamma values for the association between region and the "above" and "below" classification were .03,.10, .01, and .17 on, respectively, the white and nonwhite dropout and white and nonwhite adult illiteracy variables.

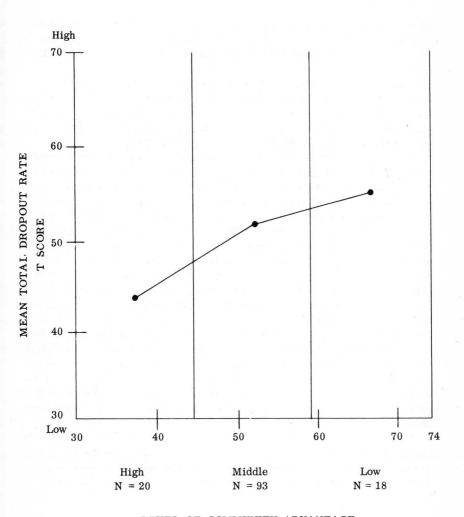

Figure 4-1
RELATIONSHIP BETWEEN AVERAGE LEVEL OF COMMUNITY
ADVANTAGE AND MEAN TOTAL DROPOUT RATE
FOR 131 CITIES

Review of Correlates

LET us review very briefly the correlates for each variable, acknow-
ledging at this point only that we have a pattern but no *neat* package in
which the same variable will do for any two or three dependent variables.

Cities with a high white dropout rate tended to be those with
smaller rather than larger white collar work forces, declining or
static rather than expanding populations, and higher numbers of very
poor families relative to population size. These factors alone account
for nearly half the variation across cities in dropout rates.

To make our point even clearer, we have reduced the main relation
to a line chart in Figure 4-1. Here, we have combined the nonwhite
and the white dropout rates into a single total dropout rate, as indicated on the vertical axis. Along the horizontal axis, we clustered
cities which exhibited high scale scores on percent of families with
incomes of less than $1,000 in 1960, percent of local labor force com-
posed of male laborers, the nonworker ratio (see Appendix B), and
percent of occupied housing units with more than 1.01 persons per
room. Table 4-2 presents the zero order r's between these four variables. This Table indicates that all of the variables show a mild positive relationship, but that none of the variables are very strongly interrelated. In short, our crude index of Community Advantage consists of four combinable indices of poverty, occupational mix, underemployment, and overcrowding. Clearly, a general linear relation obtains: the lower the level of advantage within a great city, the higher
that city's dropout rate relative to others. (This type of presentation
confounds variables and leads to spurious correlations, but here it *is*
clear and it summarizes what we have assessed with precision earlier.)

The interpretation is similar between the two dependent variables,
but far from identical. High school withdrawal is sensitive to emerging economic conditions and prospects, while adult illiteracy is a
cumulative but *past* condition. The high school dropout withdraws

Table 4-2
Correlation Matrix of Variables Included in Index of Community Advantage

Variables	% Units With More 1.01 Per Room	% Families Income Less $1,000	% Male Laborers
% Families Income less $1,000	.46		
% Male Laborers	.47	.57	
Nonworker Ratio	.41	.27	.25

under the structural constraints of a social and economic context of low advantage. Functionally illiterate adults comprise the *least* mobile segment of the adult population — the segment that stays on in a city long after the labor market there has deteriorated and long after wage earners with higher educational attainments have left for new urban frontiers. The two educational conditions are associated, yet a city might strengthen its context of advantage, hence reducing its dropout rate, while its accumulated number of poorly or very incompletely schooled adults remained high. At the extremes only, therefore, is the association strong.

Cities with a high nonwhite dropout rate contain fewer wealthy or well-to-do nonwhite families, higher proportions of nonwhite unskilled workers as well as adult illiterates (both white and nonwhite) and more white dropouts. Also, the deviant case analysis suggests similar patterns for accounting for both white and nonwhite cities exhibiting higher or lower dropout rates than expected, with one exception. This was that AFDC levels of expenditure are correlated with lower-than-expected levels of white school withdrawal but with higher-than-expected levels for nonwhites.

In this study, we considered a wide range of explanatory variables, most of them, however, being direct indicators of population characteristics, social or economic. The deviant case analysis might well have been expanded to include more, for we got some clues that relative levels of municipal expenditures on human services are associated with levels of school withdrawal and attainment. We had hoped that we might secure meaningful *qualitative* evidence that cities deviated from the expected as a function of special programming efforts in education and welfare services, but as with our hypothesis that some *regional* effects would be reflected, none of the qualitative information we managed to obtain indicated anything of significance.

Interpretation

INDEED, the correlational pattern was plain enough without elaborate exploration of deviant cases. This pattern is one in which the odds that militate against graduating from high school for any given American adolescent vary notably from community to community, and these odds are in turn mainly a function of the odds militating against demographic and economic *growth* for any given community. No doubt there are important psychological and educational determinants of withdrawal from high school. But in the aggregate, withdrawal is associated more relevantly with the growth prospects present not in the student but in the city he inhabits (Miller, Saleem & Harrington, p. 71-77).

A static or stagnant big city, relative to others at least, will be one that is growing much more slowly or is declining faster than comparable communities. As new centers of opportunity open up, better educated, more mobile adults and their households will migrate to them. Centers with no rising prospects will accumulate less well educated adults. And, as local prospects become depressed further, this condition of the setting will depress the level of graduation from high school among adolescents.

Few cities are vulnerable on all four of our educational indicators, just as the economic and demographic prospects before most great urban centers were complicated or mixed, as of 1959. Our multiple regression suggests that a range of factors must be considered before the specific vulnerabilities emerge for inspection and analysis. Nevertheless, the gross *correspondence* between a cluster of correlates for one dependent variable and the cluster for any other provides our reason for terming the general pattern plain enough to see.

ADULT FUNCTIONAL ILLITERACY

OUR analysis has also supported our hypothesis about the proportion of adults with very low educational attainment per large city. We found that cities with high rates of white in-migration and with occupational mixtures that contained a larger proportion of white collar (e.g., advantaged) jobs, were cities with relatively *low* numbers of functionally illiterate adults. And, cities with relatively smaller numbers of menial as opposed to other work for nonwhites and with lower levels of pervasive poverty in nonwhite households, were cities with relatively *low* numbers of functionally illiterate nonwhite adults. Rates of in-migration, poverty, and occupational opportunity were in fact common to both white and nonwhite correlations.

Again, to make the matter quite clear, we have supplied a graphic summary in Figure 4-2. Here, the vertical axis scales combined (white with nonwhite) levels of low adult educational attainment, while the vertical axis combines indicators of poverty, occupational mix, underemployment, and overcrowding. The linear association is even more definite than in the high school dropout graph, particularly since cities with the very poorest economic prospects reflected a mean T score of 62 in this figure — a sharp peak, indeed.

THE LINK BETWEEN EDUCATIONAL ATTAINMENT AND EMPLOYMENT SECURITY RESTATED

A YOUNG man's ability to secure a job and thus to earn a wage depends more and more each year upon his schooling. The correlation is obvious to all, as we said in Chapter 1, but why is it increasing? There are two main structural explanations: growth in the younger labor force and a changing mix of occupations.

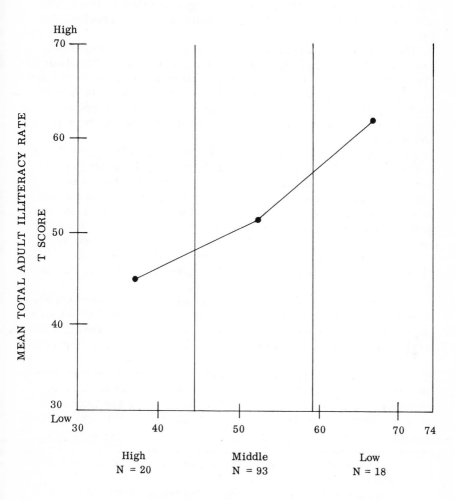

Figure 4-2
RELATIONSHIP BETWEEN AVERAGE LEVEL OF COMMUNITY
ADVANTAGE AND MEAN TOTAL ADULT ILLITERACY RATE
FOR 131 CITIES

The net increase in young persons under 25 in the work force will equal 6.2 million between 1960 and 1970. This contrasts with a net increase of 400,000 in the same age group from 1950 to 1960. The present growth is thus more than 15 times that of the previous decade.

The occupational structure has, in the meanwhile, changed in a way that further complicates change in the work force. For about 30 years, the economy has changed from dependence upon a "cheap and abundant" goods-producing work force composed mainly of factory workers and farm workers, to dependence upon service-producing workers who must be more skilled or trainable, however high-priced and scarce.

About 56% of the work force produced goods in 1930. This fraction dwindled to 44% by 1960. Within this shift, the job market changed even more emphatically within the historic central cities of the nation. There, the market moved in the same fashion, but at a more drastic pace and at a time when the in-migration to cities was reaching a peak. For example, New York City lost 84,000 jobs in the manufacturing field between 1959 and 1963. In the same period, New York City gained 69,000 jobs in service fields, 45,000 in government, and 21,000 in finance, insurance, and real estate. All of this is an extension of the longer trend *away* from agriculture.

The high school dropout was never much of an economic liability on the farm. For this and other reasons, the rural level of school attainment has long been below the urban. Since 1945, however, a net total of about 2 million farm workers have left rural areas each decade to seek work in cities. This cityward movement of less educated job seekers, while it has been going on since 1910, intensified over just these postwar years when unskilled jobs in urban as in rural areas were *shrinking*. Employment of professional and technical workers increased by 47% between 1950 and 1960. This was a growth rate more than three times greater than that for all occupational groups taken together. Most of this growth, and nearly all of the 34% increase in clerical workers over the same period, occurred solely in metropolitan areas.

It is apparent that the expanding occupational sectors in the national economy are those requiring very high levels of formal education. The fastest shrinking sectors are those best suited for those with weaker school credentials. The entire process, moreover, is compounded by the cityward migration of rural families and youth ill-trained for the emerging market of employment. The high school dropouts make up a large and growing share of that part of the work force which is static, shrinking, or expanding least rapidly.

This tightening dilemma takes place against a backdrop of heightening educational attainment for the adult population as a whole. In 1940, for example, nearly 70% of all American workers were *without*

high school diplomas. By 1962, this proportion had declined to 46%.
The dropout and the adult with no more than a grade school education
become more visible, hence socially and economically more problematical. They are at once more and more atypical, yet less and less
employable.

More Interpretation

TECHNOLOGICAL transformation, cityward migration and related
urbanizing forces, and such matters as changing educational and welfare requirements are ecologically patterned and even "determined."
As technologies change, American society grows continually in complexity and scale. Within this overall growth, however, delicate yet
significant geographic, economic and demographic forces operate to
check and balance, or to inflate and depress one another systematically.

The big cities in our sample are nested, for the most part, in increasingly distinct regional or metropolitan area economies. Each is
a center for an area differentiated by way of goods and services produced, distributed, or stored there, from most other centers in the
national society. Each also is economically integrated through this
differentiation with the national economy and for the great cities, with
the *world* economic community. These big cities grow at different
rates. The economic division within which they operate is only indi-
rectly cooperative. For the most part, it is fiercely competitive.
Regional economic growth in one metropolitan area tends to occur at
the expense of growth in *less* effectively competitive metropolitan
areas elsewhere in the nation.

This patterning is well understood. What our work does, however,
is to extend the implication of the process to linked but less well understood phenomena. For example, migration occurs chiefly in response to changes in the urban loci of advantage. This overall urban
migratory process affects profoundly the residual population characteristics, and hence the institutions that shape and serve these characteristics.

A large community in decline may not only come to sustain a larger
per capita burden of welfare and related municipal services. It will
also lag in the deeper sense that the decline may increase costs in the
public sector at the same time it stimulates an increase in school
failure or withdrawal. As the process lengthens, moreover, the proportion of educationally less advantaged adults increases as the better
educated migrate to growing areas.

We see no reason to conceive of this pattern as *determined* economically or ecologically. A major resource for metropolitan area
change, after all, is social organization and the subcultural capacity
to innovate competitively. Thus, the historical counter to economic

determinism applies here. The declining or static cities are probably also those where investments in human resources through social and educational services are truncated or were of poor quality over a long period of two to three generations. In brief, the relationships are reciprocal.

To explore this, we queried relevant local public agencies in big cities that deviated from expectancy on either dependent variable (see Appendix B for forms). We asked about educational and welfare programs *designed* to remedy or cope with problems of high school withdrawal, adult illiteracy, and welfare dependency. We predicted that the deviant communities would differ in the extent or quality of their educational and welfare services and programs. Cities with far fewer dropouts than expected would maintain more outstanding preventive or rehabilitative programs, for example, than those with excessive dropouts.

We found *no* relationship obtained between our educational variables of dropout and illiteracy and the qualitative data on school and welfare programs. This was consistent, incidentally, with our findings of no relation between *region* (or culture area) and either dependent variable among the deviant cities.

The finding may be illustrated this way. The city of Louisville had a much *higher* than average school dropout rate. It also maintains, and indeed maintained prior to 1959, several outstanding educational programs intended to reduce the rate. It has a diligent guidance staff trained to help prevent school withdrawal. It has a continuing education program that includes a high school diploma program and many relevant types of job training. Moreover, the regular instructional programs of Louisville's secondary schools are differentiated along advanced academic, general, basic, and special educational "tracks." In spite of these services, or perhaps in conjunction or harmony with them, the total dropout rate by our measure was a high one — 80, or 3 standard deviations from the big city mean of 50. Most crucially, Louisville was a city of comparatively *poor* economic opportunity in 1960.

The city of Dearborn, Michigan, in contrast, had a total dropout rate of 26 by our measure, or more than 2 standard deviations *lower* than average for the 131 cities. Yet Dearborn has most of the educational programs and services to be found in Louisville, including flexibility of curriculum, industrial education sequences, group guidance, and summer school offerings. The difference between Louisville and Dearborn is not in their services, we believe, but in their levels of community advantage. Where Louisville was significantly below average on our measure of community advantage, Dearborn was significantly *above*.

In our judgment, then, the economic context is fairly determinative! The educational and welfare services we looked into and summarized for all deviant case communities, for one thing, are in sum in no sense proportionate to the scale of need. In a very large city such as New York or Chicago, for example, from 100,000 to 400,000 citizens may be welfare dependents at any time. The number of citizens living at the same level of insecurity, moreover, is about twice that large. For New York City, for example, this means that in 1963, at least one million persons suffered economic deprivation.

Public services through schools and public welfare are nowhere commensurate with urban needs in either scope or relevance. Only a fraction of the insecure adult and late adolescent population is served publically *in any way*, and the services rendered are not of a kind that will offer the recipient a substantially improved opportunity for security. Therefore, with minor departures from the pattern, wage earning prospects in the primarily private sector of urban regional economies must be the dog that wags the tail of school holding power.

PROGRAM IMPLICATIONS

HEALTH, education, and welfare expenditures, other vital factors being held constant, are generally related unfavorably to current levels of educational attainment. In other words, cities with *higher* levels of nonwhite school dropouts and adult illiterates than one would be led to expect from pertinent social and economic conditions, are cities with *higher* than average per pupil and per family AFDC expenditures. They are also cities that spend relatively *more* on health services.

In the partial model implied by our analysis, then, the public sectors of the municipal economy (including some of those with state and Federal sources) do not equalize, and usually fail to so much as *compensate* for differences in life prospects, let alone to remedy problems or strengthen opportunity.

One of our aims in undertaking this study was to illuminate the bases on which public programs are designed and maintained to combat income insecurity. We have spoken to this issue thus far in at least three ways. First, we have concluded from empirical analysis that health, education, and public welfare expenditures — other socioeconomic factors held constant — are generally unfavorably associated with levels of school withdrawal and adult illiteracy. That is, cities with higher proportions of dropouts and illiterates than expected tend to be cities with *higher* than average educational, health, and public welfare expenditures.

Secondly, we have concluded that no observable association obtains between *character* of educational or welfare programs and levels of school withdrawal and adult illiteracy. Third, we have suggested that the public sectors of American municipal economies do not equalize,

and usually fail to so much as *compensate* slightly for gross differences in life prospects, let alone remedy insecurities or strengthen
individual opportunities. We have suggested this in view of the insuf-
ficiency of public supports when contrasted with the size of the chal-
lenge.

In pursuing this reasoning, however, and in emphasizing the determinative role of the economic context, we have no intention of avoid-
ing *sociological* features of welfare programming. We are not, for
instance, depicting the economic context of big cities as a matter of
mere surplus or of relative deficiency in aggregate demand. This may
be the case, to be sure. It may be that "stagnant" or low advantage
cities are those situated in regional economies where demand is defi-
cient solely because investment has not risen rapidly enough. (It is
important to recall that our data precede the period of the 1963 tax
cut, which appears to have demonstrated the force for economic
growth generated when Federal budget surpluses cease to restrain investment. We assume that the new growth has modified the context of
opportunity in at least several of the cities that were so stagnant as
of 1960.)

But our data, and our interpretation, emphasize not so much the
concept of demand as the concept of the ecology of the labor market.
We began with a concern with income insecurity among youths and un-
dereducated adults. Our concern was therefore with the social implications of the failure of urban employment to expand even as urban
output continues to expand. Our concern is with the progressive elimination of unskilled and semiskilled jobs by computers and general
automation. It centers upon the resulting ever-higher educational requirements that underlie steady employment.

We believe that the reduction of deficiencies in aggregate economic
demand, as through a tax cut, will have little durable bearing upon the
problems of poverty and dependency. In the big cities, these would
have to be attacked directly through programs of vocational education,
job retraining, urban redevelopment, concerted social services, re-
habilitation, and improved benefits under extended social insurance.
Important as they may be, in our view tax reduction and other investment and demand stimulating strategies may have little to do with as-
sisting the unemployed young or the displaced adult worker.

It is extremely difficult for the sociological imagination to envisage
programs adequate to the magnitude of the occasion. For example, it
took public agencies in New York City many months during 1964 and
early 1965 to arrange to open about 24 offices to receive applicants
for 900 part time and 4,500 full time jobs, under the new Neighborhood Youth Corps program. This program was intended specifically
as an aid to high school dropouts, yet it would not affect the total
dropout population if it were magnified fivefold. Furthermore, it is
hard to grasp how it could be magnified at all, or even repeated in a

second and third year of operations insofar as about 40% of the jobs being offered are for posts in city departments.[2]

Or take as illustration the Chicago Literacy Program. Based on the premise that actual illiteracy among selected adult populations of Chicago was 51% rather than the 7% indicated by reported completion of a fifth grade education, the Cook County Department of Public Aid began in 1962 to cooperate energetically with the Chicago Board of Education in a program of reading instruction for welfare recipients. The program has been evaluated as effective and its essentials are being introduced into East St. Louis (Ziegler, 1963; Brooks, 1964).

These are worthwhile programs, but their prospects as solutions to adult illiteracy and income insecurity are dismal if not nil. If we accept the findings of the Chicago and East St. Louis studies as fairly valid, of the one-fourth of all adults who are welfare dependents in these cities, over half are unable to read at the fifth grade level. For either city, the resulting instructional clientele would exceed the number of children and youth requiring public education in any one year. For prompt educational action in a situation described by the Cook County Department of Public Aid as "a desperate social drag race with a fast moving urban giant [automation]," literacy training would have to be dispensed to hundreds of thousands of adults in a single city within less than a decade. The Chicago Literacy Program prescribes obligatory attendance at "social classrooms" for illiterate welfare recipients, but its program cannot be extended beyond limited neighborhoods — its current pilot application — without vast local and state and public expenditures, if then.

Most problematical, moreover, is the circular fallacy inherent in such programs, if our findings have any validity. There may be a limited number of jobs available for newly literate adults fresh out of pilot programs in literacy training. But they are very apt to be like the jobs available in New York City for dropouts: scarce in number and good for one filling per generation. If students withdraw from high school when work prospects are poor, will adults take literacy training seriously if jobs are not the reward for the effort?

CONCLUDING SPECULATION

COMMUNITY action programs, innovations in welfare and educational services, training and retraining programs, are all helpful and relevant. The attempts they entail often set in motion many other quests for political and economic solutions to insecurity, and some of these

---

[2]There are, of course, policy alternatives that would lead to solution of the problem. For an inventory, see Gans (1964).

may prove efficacious. Also, education-centered efforts in welfare may have value for the vitality of welfare agencies, somewhat apart from manifest outcomes. That is to say, unless programs endure, the ability of welfare agencies to adapt will be impaired. Programs that in some respects do not work must be maintained, and changed periodically, or the very formal organizational machinery for doing anything will grow inflexible or will disappear.

It is hard to imagine these arguments proving persuasive in the public marketplace of program proposals and fiscal sponsorship, however. The burden of our research is that existing welfare and education programs in the big cities do not affect levels of school withdrawal. The educational barriers to economic security are not surmounted by the efficacy or scope of existing welfare or welfare-related educational efforts in the public sector of the economy. Even the relative distribution of these barriers in the big cities, in fact, is generally not affected.

If this monograph has an implication for welfare and social security programming in general, it seems to us to be that the time when programs could be tied to employability has come to an end. Major national policies to the contrary notwithstanding, we are approaching the end of an era of trying to equip men and women to move from the welfare roll to the payroll. The new era seems to be one in which we will disabuse ourselves, by virtue of the problems of our major urban centers, that educational programs can resolve welfare or employment problems, or vice versa.

Even increased economic growth in some big cities will not resolve welfare problems in others. Welfare and social security programming should come, ideally, to be articulated with the character of the national and metropolitan area economies. Educational barriers to security are real when opportunities are limited. Therefore, compensation and protection against changing contingencies will have to be developed for citizens in areas and communities suffering tightening limitations. These are dynamic in ways that programs to prevent dropouts and programs to teach adults to read can never be. Such programs are nowhere as pertinent as unemployment insurance, disability insurance, and other forms of social insurance (perhaps in the French tradition) that can transcend local variations, yet compensate protectively in periods of insecurity.

Our speculation is that local welfare programs are of value as stimuli for change, as publicity for challenges, and as contributions to social service. But the combination essential for the elimination of educational barriers to economic security is the combination of increased economic growth for urban communities on the one hand and increased, more diversified social insurance for individuals and households on the other.

PROCEDURES
AND
MEASURES

THE PURPOSE OF THIS STUDY was to identify the extent, distribution, and social and economic correlates of functional illiteracy among adults and withdrawal from high school among youths, across the largest cities in the United States.

The first major task was specification of the dependent variables. The customary index of functional illiteracy is adults reporting less than five years of elementary schooling in the decennial census. Although a recent study (Brooks, 1962) raised doubts about the accuracy of this index, consideration of the problem led us to conclude that for the analysis of aggregate populations, functional illiteracy among adults may be estimated from grade completed in school.[1]

---

[1]Deton Brooks tested welfare recipients directly for literacy and then compared illiteracy as measured by an achievement test, with illiteracy as estimated by level of formal education. The results were discrepant, leading the investigator to conclude that reported last grade in school is a poor indicator of actual reading achievement. What this investigator neglected in the course of demonstrating that many individuals reporting more than four years of formal schooling are, in fact, functionally illiterate, however, is the fact that the gross association between educational level and tested literacy is $r = .51$ (N:198, p less than .001). The discrepancies center among those with more than four years of schooling who nonetheless test out as illiterate or near illiterate. Among those with less than five years of schooling, 40 percent tested as illiterate or below third grade reading norms. About 72 percent of the same uneducated group tested as less literate than the nation's fourth graders. These factors, and the lack of another suitable measure, led

There is no conventional index of high school withdrawal. Two of the more common measures employed are (1) the comparison of the 9th grade high school membership to the number graduating three years later; and (2) the computation of the ratio of high school graduates to the number of 18-year-olds resident in the community. Both of these methods are subject to the same sources of error: they fail to account for transfer in or out of a school system, and for school grade retardation and acceleration. Since these types of errors form the largest part of the category of "involuntary withdrawals" and, therefore, inflate the dropout rate greatly, we decided against employing them in this study.

The more reliable methods of computing high school withdrawal rates that have been used in the past proved unrealistic for a large cross-city comparison. These methods involve the careful study of a given school or schools, and the tracing of each individual in the population either for one year, in the annual methods, or for a number of years (with subsequent adjustments being made in the base and true membership of the class), for the longitudinal methods (Segal & Schwarm, 1957). The number and size of the cities and high schools involved in our study, and time considerations, led us to the conclusion that these types of methods were unfeasible.

Originally we proposed to secure official estimates of withdrawal directly by mail from state and city departments of education, adjusting the estimates where necessary, to correspond to the technique employed by the United States Office of Education in 1957 (Segal & Schwarm, 1957). After studying the dropout problem in general, and consulting with various associates, we found that one of the major problems in this area is the lack of uniformity in reporting statistics dealing with school retention and withdrawal. Many cities do not compile these figures in a usable form. This factor, together with the normal expectation of some refusals concerning cooperation, led us to use Census data for the computation of our dropout rates.

Table 101 of the *1960 U.S. Census of Population* provides enrollment figures by grade, while Table 102 presents data on the number of persons *not* enrolled in school by the last grade completed. Both tables are broken down by age, sex and color. These data were available in published form, or on tape, for all cities containing 100,000 or more persons, and a few smaller cities that are central cities of Standard Metropolitan Statistical Areas (SMSA). To arrive at specific dropout rates, we divided the number of dropouts (persons *not* enrolled in school who had completed grades 8, 9, 10, or 11) by the "total population" (those enrolled in high school plus those not enrolled in school who had completed the above mentioned grades). The data

us to use the customary census index of adult functional illiteracy in this study.

were compiled for the population aged 14 to 19, as the high school population is between the ages of 14 and 18, and we allowed for one year of retardation. Grade 8 was used as the lower cutting off point because the major concern of this study was "high school" withdrawal. We are not saying that a ratio for lower levels could not be employed; it is, however, an option we did not utilize. Two procedures were employed here to determine what effect this cutoff point would have on our dropout rates. First, for the 20 largest cities we computed a dropout rate for the nonwhite population based on an earlier grade ratio. The numerator here was the nonwhite population not enrolled in school who had completed six or seven grades of education. The denominator became the nonwhite population not enrolled in school who had completed the above mentioned grades, plus the nonwhite population enrolled in grades 7 and 8. The same age break was employed. We then correlated this earlier dropout rate with the rate obtained for the nonwhite population for grades 8 - 11. The resulting Pearsonian r = .74 (significant beyond .01 level). The results of this correlation showed the similarity between the dropout rates for the 20 cities for earlier and later grades; those cities showing high rates on one measure would tend to show high rates on the other, etc. Therefore, the 8th grade cutoff would not distort our specific dropout rates. Secondly, to again check the validity of our dropout rates computed by the above method, we correlated our total rates with those computed by Daniel Schreiber in his study *Holding Power/Large City School Systems*. His rates were computed by a more customary method employed by the U.S. Office of Education (Schreiber, 1964). Data were available for 109 of our sample cities and the resulting Pearsonian r = .62 (significant beyond .01 level). Both of these procedures supported the use of the above index of high school withdrawal.

The general equation for computation of dropout rates reads as follows: where X is the specific dropout rate, A is the number not enrolled in high school who completed between grades 8 to 11 of education, and B is the number enrolled in high school: $X = A/(A + B)$.

The advantages of using Census data, compared to all the past methods of computations, greatly outweighted the possible limitations imposed by the inadequacies of Census information in general. By using Census information, we were assured of arriving at uniform rates for *all* the cities in our sample; the possible effects of different methods of compiling and reporting retention and withdrawal figures were eliminated. One of the largest sources of error in computing dropout rates—the effect of migration—was eliminated. Our "total population" by delineation became all the 14 to 19 year olds either enrolled in high school or not enrolled in school, but having finished between grades 8 to 11 of education. Since our figures were not based on individual schools, and by definition all of the persons were residents of the given city, the effects of transfers in and out of a given school system and migration, in general, were eliminated.[2] In addition, the use of Census data eliminated acceleration and retardation as possible sources of error. Children who accelerated, finished high school and then secured a job or went on to college, would not enter into our sample since they did not fall into the enrolled or non-enrolled groups. Those children who were retarded would be included in our sample and not considered dropouts while they were still enrolled in school. Finally, the use of Census data permitted subsequent repetition of this study and a basis for standardization of dropout studies in all large communities.

We felt that these advantages justified our use of Census material, even when the limitations of Census information were considered. Although Census data are not completely reliable, due to errors in enumeration, reporting, and to the generalization of some results from a 25% probability sample, it was felt that these errors would be randomly distributed across all of the cities. Since the main aim of this study was a *comparative* statement concerning dropout rates in light of given rates for each of our sample cities, the errors inherent would be of little importance, and would not hinder our study. Furthermore, it was apparent that the same types of errors of reporting and recording information would be present if another method or source was utilized, with the compounding effects of non-uniform statistics.

Having specified our dependent variables in general form, our next major step was to select the sample and then to further refine our dependent variables.

Originally we intended to include all cities of the continental United States, containing 80,000 or more persons, in our sample. This, we believed, would have taken in all the large urban centers — 80,000 being the limit of large, rather than medium size cities. The decision to use Census data in the computation of our dropout rates, however, caused us to limit our sample. The data we needed was available for all of the cities containing 100,000 or more persons in 1960 (129) and for only 13 cities between 80,000 and 100,000 population, that were central cities of SMSA. This resulted in a total of 142 cities. Preliminary inspection of the dropout rates for the 50 largest cities, containing 250,000 or more persons, led us to eliminate 11 of the original 142 cities. These cities had 10 percent or more of their population in the armed forces. The cities so eliminated and their percentage of males in the armed forces are indicated in Table A-1.

Of the 50 largest cities, the male dropout rates for only three were out of line with the rest: San Diego had a 50.4% male rate, Long Beach, 34.0%, and Norfolk, 46.8%. When these cities were looked at closely, all three showed a great excess of males aged 17 to 19 over females of this age group. The only factor that would seem to account

---

[2]Since Residence was determined on April 1st and School Enrollment as of February 1st, some migration effects might still be present.

Table A-1
Cities with 10 Percent or More of Their Male Population in the Armed Forces

City	Percent of Males in Armed Forces
Montogomery, Ala.	11.6
Long Beach, Calif.	17.1
San Diego, Calif.	29.4
Columbus, Georgia	22.5
Savannah, Georgia	10.0
Amarillo, Texas	19.7
El Paso, Texas	15.5
Wichita Falls, Texas	25.4
Newport News, Virginia	20.8
Norfolk, Virginia	38.2
Portsmouth, Virginia	24.7

for this aɴu for the disproportionately high dropout rates was the number of males in the armed forces.[3] When the population figures were checked (taking employment data and adding the number in the civilian labor force and the number in the armed forces), the military personnel were included in the population figures, even though their permanent residences, in many cases, are probably elsewhere.

In order to prevent contamination of our results by this factor, we eliminated all cities with 10 percent or more of the male population aged 14 or over in the armed forces. The decision to use a 10 percent criterion resulted from the computation of the percent in the armed forces for all 142 cities (see Table A-2). The "natural break" occurs between the lowest in the 10 percent or more category — Savannah with 10 percent — and the highest in the 5.0 - 9.9% group — Topeka with 7.2% in the armed forces. The elimination of these 11 cities left us with our final sample, N = 131. This sample covers almost every state in the continental United States and every region in the country.

Originally, we intended to use sex in reporting our dropout rates, as well as race, on both dependent variables. Race was considered

---

[3]Enlistment in the armed forces has been indicated by many sources as one of the major reasons of withdrawal from high school. In a *New Look at School Dropouts*, the U.S. Department of Health, Education and Welfare listed this reason as accounting for 6% of the country's dropouts, and indicated that this was probably understated. In a 1961 study of St. Paul, Minnesota, 12.7% of the boy dropouts gave this as their reason for withdrawal, while in Ohio the figure was 22.1% (Sofokidis & Sullivan, 1964, p. xvi; Johnson & Sagert, 1961, p. 55; Nachman, Getson, & Odgers, 1963, p. 31).

Table A-2

Frequency Distribution of Percent of Male Population 14 and Over in the
Armed Forces for Original Sample Cities

Percent of Males in Armed Forces	Number of Cities
10.0 or over	11
5.0-9.9	8
2.0-4.9	19
1.0-1.9	13
Under 1.0	91
Total	142

important due to indications of large differences between whites and
nonwhites in past research. A sex break on adult functional illiteracy
was impossible, however, due to lack of information. The Census does
not use sex as a control on this variable for the nonwhite population
and therefore it was not possible to get white and nonwhite sex breaks.
However, it was possible to use sex as a control in computing our
dropout rates, and available literature in the field pointed to the need
for this procedure. Therefore, in the computation of the dropout rates
for the 50 largest cities, we used sex as well as race in specification
of our dropout rates.

Preliminary inspection of the dropout rates for these 50 cities
yielded surprising results. With few exceptions, the female rate was
consistently higher than the male rate. We therefore undertook a
careful analysis of our method of computation and the data upon which
our computations rested.

The procedure we employed in this analysis was to take two cities
in which the female rate was higher — Los Angeles (third largest
city) and Tulsa (49th largest city) — and look at both components,
enrollment and non-enrollment, by age and sex. By so doing, some
of the possible reasons behind the trend became apparent.

The first possible reason for a higher female dropout rate was

Table A-3

Number Enrolled in High School by Sex for Los Angeles and Tulsa

City	Sex		Total
	Male	Female	
Los Angeles	55,533	53,758	109,291
Tulsa	6,351	6,318	12,669

Table A-4
Base Membership in High School According to Sex and Size of City[a]

| Size of City | Sex | | Total |
	Male	Female	
Grp A Cities[b]	61,721	61,564	123,285
Grp B Cities[c]	183,097	173,059	356,156

[a]Based on Table A-1, Segel and Schwarm, *Retention in High Schools in Large Cities* (1957).
[b]Cities with population from 200,000 to 1,000,000.
[c]Cities with population of over 1,000,000.

revealed in the enrollment data. Numerically, there are slightly more males than females enrolled in high school. This difference does not seem to be a peculiarity of Census data, since Segel and Schwarm (1957) showed the same trend. Although the difference is not very large, the pattern takes on increasing importance when the enrollment figures are broken down by age (Table A-5) and when the number of students in high school at each age level are percentaged over the population for that age (Table A-6).

From these two tables we can see that the predominance of males in high school is not consistent. In the 14 year old age group, a higher percent of the female population is enrolled in school, compared to the male population, and more of the 14 year olds in school are females. Although the differences in the other age groups (with one small exception in Tulsa) are all in favor of males, that is they

Table A-5
Percent of High School Enrollement by Sex According to Age for Los Angeles and Tulsa

| Age | City | | | | | |
| | Los Angeles | | | Tulsa | | |
	Males	Females	N	Males	Females	N
14	47.9	52.1	23,153	44.3	55.7	1,820
15	50.8	49.2	28,244	50.8	49.2	3,139
16	51.6	48.4	27,502	49.9	50.1	3,369
17	51.0	49.0	21,801	51.3	48.7	2,934
18	56.2	43.8	6,380	54.0	46.0	1,158
19	54.0	46.0	2,211	55.0	45.0	249

Table A-6
Percent of All Males and Females of a Given Age Enrolled in High School for
Los Angeles and Tulsa

Age	City			
	Los Angeles		Tulsa	
	Males	Females	Males	Females
14	69.2	75.8	44.6	52.4
15	91.5	88.8	85.1	83.7
16	91.2	85.5	93.5	85.5
17	73.4	66.5	85.6	77.7
18	27.2	19.0	47.1	30.7
19	10.1	7.0	12.1	6.9

predominate on both indicators of enrollment, the differences displayed are of varying magnitude, with the 18 and 19 age groups
showing the largest male predominance. These differences in enrollment, according to age, suggest that females start high school earlier
and finish school at a younger age than do males. The high school enrollment figures of the pre-fourteen age group add support to this in-
ference (Table A-7).

The effect of this on our dropout rates is a slight inflation of the
female figures and a slight reduction of the male rates for the total
group. If females do start school earlier than males, and, therefore,
leave earlier, the denominator of our dropout equation would be
affected: it would be reduced for females in the later age groups resulting in a larger percent, and increased for males in the higher
ages, causing a lower percent. Since we do not break the rates down
by age, this artifact would then affect the total group. Our dropout
rates, therefore, are in part a reflection of this different enrollment
pattern.

Even though more males than females, totally and in the older age
groups, are enrolled in high school, more females than males have

Table A-7
Number and Percent Enrolled in High School Prior to Fourteen by Sex for
Los Angeles and Tulsa

City	Sex					
	Male		Female		Total	
	N	%	N	%	N	%
Los Angeles	3,061	48.5	3,241	51.5	6,305	100.0
Tulsa	71	43.6	92	56.4	163	100.0

left school before receiving their degrees. The differences on Table A-8 are much greater than on the comparable enrollment data (see Table A A-3). The underlying factors influencing these figures are attributable to both the enrollment pattern and the nature of the Census data.

The Census data provide the number of persons aged 14-19 not enrolled in high school who have completed between grades 8 to 11 of education. Unfortunately, the Census data do not report the year in which the given individual discontinued school. Therefore, if a person left school without receiving his diploma before 1960, he would appear in this table along with the 1960 dropouts. Attendance in high school through at least age 16 is required by law in almost all large cities (Schreiber, 1964, p.65) except under unusual circumstances. Although the enforcement of this statute varies from state to state, it is more than probable that the 1960 non-enrollment figures for the 14-16 age groups are actually for 1960. However, the same statement cannot be made about the 17-19 age groups. Given the limitations of the Census data, it is possible that the 1960 non-enrollment figures for 17-year-olds include the 17-year-old dropouts in 1960 as well as the 16-year-old dropouts in 1959. Likewise, the 18-year-old group can be a composite of the overlap for 2 years, while the 19-year-old group is subjected to a possible 3-year overlap.

If the high school enrollment patterns of males and females were similar, it would be logical to assume that the possible compounding in the non-enrollment data would be equal for both sexes. However, enrollment figures seem to demonstrate that females start high school earlier than and finish before their male counterparts. Since males tend to be graduated later, and have a higher high school enrollment in the 18 and 19 age brackets, we would assume that if the non-enrollment figures were actually for one given year, namely 1960, and hence free of compounding, males should show a higher percent of non-enrollment for the 18- and 19-year-old groups. When we break down the non-enrollment figures by age and sex, we can see that this is not the case. As Table A-9 demonstrates, males show a higher percent of non-enrollment in the earlier age groups (with the exception

Table A-8
Number and Percent Not Enrolled in High School by Sex for Los Angeles and Tulsa

		Sex				
	Male		Female		Total	
City	N	%	N	%	N	%
Los Angeles	8,788	45.6	10,468	54.4	19,256	100.0
Tulsa	639	30.5	1,457	69.5	2,096	100.0

Table A-9
Percent of Males and Females Not Enrolled in High School
by Age for Los Angeles and Tulsa

| | City | | | |
| | Los Angeles | | Tulsa | |
Age	Male	Female	Male	Female
14	4.9	4.5	5.6	4.1
15	7.3	6.6	10.2	5.1
16	13.6	13.7	13.8	15.4
17	21.4	20.0	21.1	19.6
18	25.1	25.1	21.0	28.6
19	27.7	30.0	28.3	27.1
Total	100.0	99.9	100.0	99.9
N	8,788	10,468	639	1,457

of 16) as compared to females, and show a lower percent of non-enrollment in either the 18-year-old group (Tulsa) or the 19-year-old
group (Los Angeles). This pattern is, of course, the opposite of that
displayed on the enrollment data, and becomes interesting when
viewed in light of the dropout rates themselves.

In light of the above discussion of the non-enrollment data, as well
as the conflicting enrollment patterns, the dropout rates take on increased importance when they are broken down by age. Although females show a consistently higher dropout rate for each age, the difference between the sexes is extremely slight in the earlier ages, and

Table A-10
Percent of Dropouts According to Age and Sex for Los
Angeles and Tulsa

| | City | | | |
| | Los Angeles | | Tulsa | |
Age	Male	Female	Male	Female
14	0.7	0.7	0.5	0.8
15	1.0	1.1	0.9	0.9
16	1.9	2.2	1.3	2.9
17	2.9	3.3	1.9	3.7
18	3.4	4.1	1.9	5.4
19	3.8	4.9	2.6	5.1
Total	13.7	16.3	9.1	18.8

reaches a peak in the later age groups where discrepancies exist in the enrollment and non-enrollment figures.

The pattern displayed in the enrolled data seems probable; it receives support from other sources. However, the same cannot be said of the non-enrollment figures. Here it seems as if the form of Table 102 of the Census compounds our rates in the older age groups. We cannot tell if those individuals who are not enrolled in school chose to leave in 1960 or before. From the little information we have, it seems as if many in the older age group may have left before 1960, and hence the 1960 dropout rates would be inflated since they might contain those who actually left in 1959, 1958, etc., and should not be considered *1960* dropouts. Both the enrollment and non-enrollment figures seem to indicate that this possible compounding is more prevalent among females than males, which if true would explain the higher female dropout rates.

Unfortunately, the complexity of the data prevents us from reaching definite conclusions. However, since all the cities are subjected equally to this bias, and we are more interested in comparable dropout rates than in an exact statement of the number of school leavers in a specific city, there seems to be no reason to discard the data. The similarity in the dropout rates between the sexes, when broken down by age, strongly suggests that there is not much to be gained from a male-female break. Also when a Pearsonian r was computed for a sample of 24 of the 50 largest cities, the correlation between the total male and female rates was .88. This supports the similarity of the dropout rates between the sexes. The combining of the data for both sexes would go far in reducing the possible conflicting biases in the enrollment and non-enrollment data, and prevent unreliable conclusions from being drawn in the multiple regression analysis. Therefore, the sex break was dropped from consideration, and we used only race on both dependent variables.

Race as employed in specification of our dependent variables derived from the broader classification used by the Census. This should be kept in mind when interpreting the results of the multiple regression and deviant case analysis. *Such groups as the Japanese and Chinese are included in the nonwhite classification,* although their educational patterns differ from Negroes, for example. Although the size of the nonwhite, non-Negro population is generally small in most cities, certain places, such as San Francisco, have quite a large nonwhite, non-Negro population. In these cities this factor might influence the dropout and illiteracy rates. Also, Mexicans, according to the Census definition, are classed as "white." When looking at the dropout and illiteracy rates of certain cities in the Southwestern part of the United States, this should be kept in mind.

Ideally, it would have been desirable to isolate out all of these fringe groups and use a "pure" white-Negro break on both variables;

this proved impossible in the present analysis. However, since the
effects of the present classification have importance in but a few cities, the overall picture seems quite reliable.

Data on some 50 independent variables were collected from the
Census. These dealt with most of the relevant social and economic
conditions of the cities in our sample. The variables covered in de-
tail such areas as: population and size characteristics, housing, migration and growth factors, age and sex composition, income, employment, occupation and industrial specialization data.

Where possible, these variables were collected for both the white
and nonwhite population. Tables 77 and 78 of the Census supply data
for the nonwhite population of urban places on most of the relevant
social and economic variables. By subtracting these figures from
those presented for the total population of the various cities, we were
able to obtain data for the white as well as the nonwhite group.

Seven of our sample cities were not included in Tables 77 and 78
because their nonwhite population was less than 1 percent of the total
population. These cities are: Anaheim and Glendale, California;
Dearborn, Michigan; Clifton, New Jersey; Allentown and Scranton,
Pennsylvania; and Pawtucket, Rhode Island. On those variables for
which data were collected for both the white and nonwhite population,
we assumed the nonwhite figures to be equal to zero for these cities,
and therefore used the total figures for the white. This procedure
was also employed in the computation of the nonwhite illiteracy rates.
This renders the results for these seven cities less accurate than the
other sample cities.

In computing the nonwhite dropout rates, accurate and exact information was secured, and this procedure was not employed. However,
due to the extremely small nonwhite population in these cities, it is
evident that an increase or decrease of one or two additional dropouts
will cause a much higher variation than in the other cities.

In addition to the above variables, information was secured on current per pupil expenditures (U. S. Dept. HEW, Office of Education,
1962) and various relevant city government expenditures, such as
current per capita expenditures on parks and recreation, health and
hospitals, housing and community redevelopment and public welfare.
In addition, we secured data on per capita city revenue for all cities
(U. S. Dept. of Commerce, Bureau of Census, 1961).

We were unable to secure information on current expenditures per
pupil on a city basis for one group of cities. We found that in 13 cities, the school system is defined on a county basis and therefore no
city statistics exist. These cities are: Phoenix, Arizona; Fort Lau-
derdale, Jacksonville, Miami, Orlando, St. Petersburg, and Tampa,
Florida; Baton Rouge, New Orleans, and Shreveport, Louisiana; Charlotte, North Carolina; Charleston and Huntington, West Virginia.

In these cases, county information was used in place of city data. We assume that these large cities, which contain the predominance of the county population, also receive the predominance of the county school allocation. In addition, the difference between city and county expenditures on a few cities for which both figures were present proved negligible.

Per capita city expenditures on housing and community redevelopment and public welfare were also incomplete. We could secure no data on 52 cities for the former variable, and 64 cities were missing information on the latter. We used this information, where available, but the expected importance of expenditures on public welfare for the second stage of the analysis, led us to adopt two additional independent measures for all cities: the rate and the average payment per family of Aid to Families with Dependent Children. These variables were collected for the county in which the city is located. Where the city was listed in more than one county, we used the dominant county in regard to population and geographic location of the city (U. S. Dept. HEW, Welfare Administration, 1963).

All of the above independent analytic variables as well as our dependent variables were collected for the period of 1959-1960 — this time being fixed by the *1960 Census of Population.* A complete list of all the independent variables used can be found in Table B-1 of Appendix B.

Before the analysis, we thought that it was important to convert our raw scores on all of the independent and dependent variables to a common scale. This would normalize our data, or provide a comparable reference point for all arrays of information. The T scale was adopted for this purpose. The advantage of the T scale is that it imposes a common mean of 50 and a standard deviation of 10. The calculation of T scores involves securing a frequency and a cumulative frequency distribution, determining the cumulative proportions, and then consulting a table to determine the correct T score (Edwards, 1960; Guilford, 1956). This procedure was followed for all of the variables in the study. All results reported are based on T, rather than on raw scores.

After normalizing all variables, a complete correlation matrix was generated for both the T and raw score data. We found that the correlations with dependent variables were virtually identical for both T scales and raw scores. Apparently, our raw data assumed the form of a normal distribution. However, this could not have been determined beforehand, and since the data were already transformed, the decision to use the T scores were kept. The form of the latter was also better suited to the fundamental steps of machine analysis.

The analysis stage itself was divided into two phases. The first phase involved generating, through multiple correlation and regression analysis, the best regression equation for predicting the white and nonwhite dropout and illiteracy rates, from the most highly correlated social and economic independent variables. The higher the respective multiple R obtained, the greater the accuracy of our prediction, and therefore the less chance of error. As indicated in Chapters 2 and 3, our predictions were most accurate concerning the nonwhite adult functional illiteracy rate, R = .91, and least accurate concerning the nonwhite dropout rate, R .67.

The general regression equation for a three variable problem where X^1 is the variable to be predicted, is:

$$X^1 = a + b_{12.3} X_2 + b_{13.2} X_3$$

''The 'b' coefficient gives us the slope of the regression line, and it depends upon the coefficient of correlation and the standard deviations.... The regression coefficient 'a' is a constant ... [that] assures that the mean of the predictions will equal the mean of the obtained values.'' (Guilford, 1956, p. 367)

As a result of the first stage of analysis, we were able to predict, in light of the correlated social and economic variables, white and nonwhite dropout and illiteracy rates for each of the cities in our sample. We then compared the actual and predicted rates, and classified the cities into two groups: those in which the dropout and/or illiteracy rates were identical with what one would expect in view of the city's social and economic conditions; and those in which the rates were much higher or lower than predicted from the analysis.

The cities in the first group were those in which the actual and predicted rates were the same, *plus or minus one standard error*. These cities we considered non-deviant. Those cities in which the actual rate was higher than the predicted were classified as deviant in a negative direction, and labeled ''above.'' Those in which the predicted rate was higher than the actual were considered deviant in a positive direction, and labeled ''below.'' The ''below'' cities are those having fewer dropouts or illiterates than expected from their given social and economic conditions, while the ''above'' cities have a much higher rate than expected.

The final stage of the analysis worked solely on the deviant cases in order to uncover the factors accounting for the deviance, and to discover the organizational features of communities that have coped most and least effectively with these educational barriers to economic security.

At this point, per pupil expenditures and relevant city government expenditures were introduced into the analysis to account for the residual variance. The variables introduced were dichotomized at the mean to form two groups—low (20-49 T score) and high (50-80 T score)—and were compared to the ''below'' and ''above'' cities. The resulting fourfold tables were analyzed by means of computing

Yule's Q. Q is designed to test the overall strength of a relationship
between two dichotomized variables, and varies from -1.00 to +1.00
(Mueller & Schuessler, 1961).

We also introduced *region* as a variable to attempt to account for
some of the deviance. The measure used to test the degree of association here was Gamma, the general case of Q. Gamma is interpreted
in the same way as Q, but can be applied to larger tables (Zelditch, Jr.,
1959).

In addition to the above methods, we examined the ''below'' and
''above'' cities, holding the predicted dropout and illiteracy rates constant. The procedure followed here was to compute means of all of
the independent components of the respective regression equations
and selected other variables for the ''above'' cities having a predicted
dropout or illiteracy rate of 50 or more, and to compare the means of
each variable to those for the ''below'' cities having similar predicted
rates. The same procedure was followed for the ''above'' and ''below''
cities having predicted rates of less than 50.

The results of the above procedures did not sufficiently explain the
residual variance. The means of the ''above'' and ''below'' cities,
when the predicted dropout and illiteracy rates were held constant,
were almost identical on all of the variables used. The Gamma's
computed to test regional differences were negligible. Finally, although isolated Q's were high, the pattern indicated overall absence of
associations.

Lacking results from these procedures, we tried other methods
and sources to account for the deviance. Additional information concerning peculiar local conditions and programs was secured from the
cities themselves. Two letters—one to the Superintendent of Schools
and the other to the Director of the Department of Welfare—were
sent to every deviant city. (A copy of each of these letters appears
in Appendix B.) These data, as well as information concerning age
requirements of school attendance and employment, *yielded no consistent patterns*. ''Above'' and ''below'' cities did or did not show
special interest in their dropout and illiteracy problems by instituting
programs, yet both groups of cities had varying age requirements for
leaving school and entering the labor market. Although these data
were interesting and informative, they did not satisfactorily explain
the deviance.

Finally, we returned to multiple correlation and regression analysis. Our dependent variable for this stage of the analysis was the
difference between the actual dropout and illiteracy rates obtained
from the Census, and the predicted rates obtained as the result of the
first stage of the analysis. This residual is a numerical indication of
the magnitude of the deviation, positive if the city is ''above'' and
negative if it is ''below.'' We combined the ''above'' and ''below''
cities, adding a constant to make the residual positive in all cases,

and ran two equations for each dependent variable. The use of residuals for secondary analysis has statistical precedence (Ezekiel, 1930, Chapter 14).

The first equation contained only the secondary variables — per pupil expenditures and city government items — those not included in the first analysis stage. The decision to hold these variables for secondary analysis only was based on the design of the study and our basic organizing hypotheses. However, the results of our study indicate that they might have had a primary effect, and therefore more might have been gained from introducing them in the first analysis stage. The second equation included both the primary and secondary variables and was used to supplement the findings of the first. Due to the small number of secondary variables available to us, we succeeded in explaining only a maximum of 32 percent of the possible variance on one of the dependent variables. We therefore introduced the primary variables into the equation to try and account for the remaining variance. As the discussions in Chapters 2 and 3 indicated, this procedure proved fruitful. The statistical precedent on re-using the original variables to explain the deviance is not clear. Our statistical consultation on this matter was quite mixed.

Both of these equations were run for the deviant sample alone and then separately for the non-deviant cities. On the whole, the differences between the multiple R's for both samples were quite large on each equation. We therefore concluded that the variables included in the deviant city residual were accounting for some of the deviance and that the multiple R's obtained were not mere statistical artifacts.

In order to facilitate maximum clarity in presentation, and comprehension in interpretation, we adopted a uniform method of analyzing and reporting our findings. We stopped the multiple regression correlation equation in each case where the addition of another variable reduced the F ratio below the .05 level of significance. Each text table contains all of the variables that were significantly introduced into the equation.

As indicated, a part of the first stage of analysis was concerned with predicting dropout and illiteracy rates for each city in order to determine the given city's deviant or non-deviant status. The major aspect of both stages, however, was one of explanation, of specifying the social and economic correlates of existing dropout and illiteracy rates and the conditions underlying the deviance from expected levels. The best indicator for this purpose is R^2. R^2 tells us the amount of variance in the dependent variables that is accounted for, or associated with, the independent variables in a given regression equation.

R^2 for a three variable problem can most easily be estimated from the following equation:

$$R^2{}_{1.23} = B_{12.3} r_{12} + B_{13.2} r_{13}$$

where $R^2_{1.23}$ equals the coefficient of multiple correlation, squared, between a dependent variable (X_1) and two independent variables $(X_2$ and $X_3)$, r_{12} and r_{13} equals the zero order coefficients of correlation between each independent variable separately and the dependent variable, and $B_{12.3}$ and $B_{13.2}$ are the respective Beta, or standard partial regression coefficients.

> Since the coefficient of multiple determination, or R^2, is composed of ... two components in ... [the above formula], and since each component pertains to only one of the independent variables, it is permissible to take each component as indicating the contribution of one independent variable to the total predicted variance of X_1 ... This enables us to obtain a more definite idea of the relative importance of each variable in the regression equation. (Guilford, 1956, p. 397)

For this reason all of the tables included the Beta value for each variable, the zero order r and the resulting contribution of this variable to the total predicted variance.

Use of the above equation can result in a variable making a *negative* contribution to total predicted variance if the Beta value and the zero order r have different signs. Although this can be explained mathematically, it presents considerable problems in sociological interpretation, as it is difficult to conceive that the inclusion of a variable detracts from explanation. Hence, we listed these variables in the tables without discussion. In fact, our discussion of each dependent variable centered on only a few of the major positive contributors to the total predicted variance. Inclusion of all of the variables would have added little to additional understanding, and would have resulted in considerable verbal complexity and confusion. The complete data are presented in the text tables, however, for purposes of replication, as are the actual T score values of every variable (see Appendix B).

ADDITIONAL TABLES

Table B-1
List of All Variables Used in the Study

1. Area

2. Population per Square Mile, 1960

3. Total Population, 1960

4. Percent Increase in Total Population, 1950-1960

5. Percent Nonwhite in 1960

6. Percent Nonwhite in 1950

7. Percent Increase in Nonwhite Population, 1950-1960

8. Percent Negro, 1960

9. Percent Nonwhite, Non-Negro in 1960

10. Fertility Ratio (Number of Children Under 5 per 1,000 Women 15-49)

11. Nonworker Ratio (Ratio of Persons Not in Labor Force, including children under 14, to Labor Force)

12. Percent of Total Population Under 5 Years of Age

13. Percent of Total Population Between 5-18 Years of Age

14. Percent of White Families with Income Under $ 1,000

15. Percent of White Families with Income Between $1,000-$1,999

16. Percent of White Families with Income Under $3,000

17. Percent of White Families with Income of $10,000 or More

18. Percent of Nonwhite Families with Income Under $1,000

19. Percent of Nonwhite Families with Income Between $1,000-$1,999

20. Percent of Nonwhite Families with Income Under $3,000

21. Percent of Nonwhite Families with Income of $10,000 or More

22. Percent of White Population 25 Years and Over Who Completed Less Than 5 Years of School (White Adult Functional Illiteracy Rate)

23. Percent of Nonwhite Population 25 Years and Over Who Completed Less Than 5 Years of School (Nonwhite Functional Illiteracy Rate)

24. Percent of White Civilian Labor Force, 14 and Over Who Are Unemployed

25. Percent of Nonwhite Civilian Labor Force, 14 and Over Who Are Unemployed

26. Percent of Total Employed Civilian Labor Force in White Collar Occupations (Includes Professional, Managerial [except Farm], Clerical, and Sales)

27. Percent of Housing Units, 1960, in Structures Built in 1950 or Later

28. Percent of Occupied Units With 1.01 or More Persons Per Room

29. Percent of White Population 5 Years Old and Over in 1960 Who Lived in a Different State in 1955

30. Percent of Nonwhite Population 5 Years Old and Over in 1960 Who Lived in a Different State in 1955

31. Percent of White Male Employed Population Who Are Professional, Technical and Kindred Workers

32. Percent of White Male Employed Population Who Are Operatives and Kindred Workers

33. Percent of White Male Employed Population Who Are Service Workers, Except Private Household

34. Percent of White Male Employed Population Who Are Laborers, Except Farm and Mine

35. Percent of Nonwhite Male Employed Population Who Are Professional, Technical and Kindred Workers

36. Percent of Nonwhite Male Employed Population Who Are Operatives and Kindred Workers

37. Percent of Nonwhite Male Employed Population Who Are Service Workers, Except Private Household

38. Percent of Nonwhite Male Employed Population Who Are Laborers, Except Farm and Mine

39. Percent of Nonwhite Female Employed Population Who Are Private Household Workers

40. Ratio of Males Aged 35-44 to Females Aged 35-44 (Sex Ratio)

41. Percent of Males Aged 35-44 Not in Labor Force

42. Percent of Nonwhite Females Aged 14-65, Not in Labor Force, Not in School, Not Inmates of an Institution, with Children Under 6, Husband Not Present

43. Per Pupil Expenditures, 1959-1960

44. Per Capita Expenditures on Parks and Recreation, 1960

45. Per Capita Expenditures on Health and Hospitals, 1960

46. Per Capita Revenue, 1960

47. Per Capita Expenditures on Housing and Community Redevelopment, 1960

48. Per Capita Expenditures on Public Welfare, 1960

49. Public Assistance Rate for Aid to Families with Dependent Children, 1960, for Counties in Which Cities Are Located

50. Average Payment of Aid to Families with Dependent Children, 1960, for Counties in Which Cities Are Located

51. Dropout Rate for White Population

52. Dropout Rate for Nonwhite Population

53. Median Rent

54. White Dropout Residual (Difference Between Actual and Predicted White Dropout Rates)

55. Nonwhite Dropout Residual (Difference Between Actual and Predicted Nonwhite Dropout Rates)

Key to Table B-2: T Score For Independent And Dependent Variables
Used In White Dropout Regression For 131 Sample Cities

1. Total Population in 1960

2. Increase in Total Population 1950-1960

3. Percent Negro in 1960

4. Nonworker Ratio

5. Percent of Total Population Under 5 Years of Age

6. Percent of Total Population Between 5-18 Years of Age

7. Percent of Total Employed Civilian Labor Force in White Collar
    Occupations

8. Percent of Occupied Units with 1.01 or More Persons Per Room

9. Percent of White Families with Income Under $1,000

10. Percent of White Families with Income Between $1,000-$1,999

11. Percent of White Civilian Labor Force 14 Years and Over Who
     Are Unemployed

12. Percent of White Population 25 Years and Over Who Completed
     Less than Five Years of School (White Adult Functional Illiter-
     acy)

13. Percent of White Population 5 Years and Over in 1960 Who Lived
     in a Different State in 1955

14. Percent of White Male Employed Population Who Are Laborers,
     Except Farm and Mine

15. Percent of Males 35-44 Not in Labor Force

16. Nonwhite Dropout Rate

17. White Dropout Rate - T Score

18. White Dropout Rate - Percent

Table B-2
T Score For Independent And Dependent Variables Used In White Dropout Regression For 131 Sample Cities

| City and State | T Score | | | | | | | | | | | | | | | | Dependent Variable | Raw Score |
| | Independent Variables | | | | | | | | | | | | | | | | | |
	1	2	3	4	5	6	7	8	9	10	11	12	13	14	15	16	17	18
Akron, Ohio	55	50	52	55	55	55	43	47	41	48	54	49	47	52	41	49	46	15
Albany, New York	47	43	49	43	48	43	59	37	59	57	53	53	39	62	56	46	51	17
Albuquerque, New Mexico	52	65	40	62	69	67	74	61	48	48	50	49	68	52	46	55	49	16
Allentown, Pennsylvania	42	47	38	41	40	43	42	34	44	57	47	49	39	62	53	47	51	17
Anaheim, California	40	80	32	66	69	70	61	47	44	36	50	35	67	45	35	46	41	12
Atlanta, Georgia	59	60	68	47	55	52	49	66	57	57	40	53	56	40	66	50	58	21
Austin, Texas	51	58	52	58	55	55	66	59	62	62	38	67	48	52	63	45	58	21
Baltimore, Maryland	68	47	64	50	55	55	43	53	55	48	53	59	44	52	63	56	70	25
Baton Rouge, Louisiana	48	54	62	61	62	67	55	66	44	48	48	45	56	40	53	44	41	12
Beaumont, Texas	45	55	61	60	62	64	47	61	56	48	46	49	50	40	56	45	44	14
Berkeley, California	43	44	55	36	33	31	80	37	44	57	45	41	58	45	53	31	30	08
Birmingham, Alabama	57	49	70	60	55	60	46	66	52	57	49	45	50	40	59	50	56	20
Boston, Massachusetts	63	31	49	38	48	38	49	47	52	57	52	59	44	59	59	62	61	22
Bridgeport, Connecticut	49	45	50	44	55	43	36	53	56	48	60	62	44	52	41	61	56	20
Buffalo, New York	61	38	52	53	48	48	41	41	53	57	69	55	33	64	56	57	51	17
Cambridge, Massachusetts	42	36	44	38	40	28	59	44	48	57	42	53	61	52	56	40	54	19
Camden, New Jersey	44	41	58	59	55	52	33	50	61	57	46	67	44	59	41	53	61	22
Canton, Ohio	44	44	50	57	55	52	39	50	53	57	63	55	41	69	41	50	52	18
Charleston, West Virginia	34	52	50	54	48	55	66	53	64	62	53	53	47	52	63	50	49	16

City																		
Charlotte, North Carolina	52	60	59	44	62	64	52	59	46	48	34	49	60	34	46	56	51	17
Chattanooga, Tennessee	47	47	62	58	55	60	38	62	69	64	49	62	56	52	63	50	61	22
Chicago, Illinois	74	45	58	37	55	43	46	57	44	36	45	59	44	52	56	53	54	19
Cincinnati, Ohio	61	47	56	55	55	48	42	66	59	62	50	53	50	52	53	53	70	25
Cleveland, Ohio	66	43	61	48	62	48	33	53	50	57	57	62	48	62	53	53	61	22
Clifton, New Jersey	30	56	32	39	48	52	52	37	28	28	50	55	44	45	26	30	37	11
Columbia, South Carolina	37	51	62	64	48	52	61	59	59	57	40	53	56	40	80	47	49	16
Columbus, Ohio	59	55	53	52	62	48	50	53	53	57	50	45	53	52	72	53	64	23
Corpus Christi, Texas	50	61	46	72	69	74	52	74	72	68	60	74	48	64	41	53	64	23
Dallas, Texas	63	62	55	41	62	60	57	57	50	48	35	53	54	45	46	62	61	22
Davenport, Iowa	35	53	40	52	62	55	50	55	41	48	43	35	56	62	53	47	49	16
Dayton, Ohio	55	50	56	49	55	55	43	55	50	57	53	49	50	52	46	49	56	20
Dearborn, Michigan	43	53	32	52	40	64	63	41	32	36	53	53	26	45	41	30	26	07
Denver, Colorado	60	53	46	47	55	52	63	47	46	57	41	45	63	59	46	44	58	21
Des Moines, Iowa	53	52	44	45	55	52	66	50	44	48	36	41	50	59	46	49	51	17
Detroit, Michigan	69	37	61	53	48	55	43	50	50	57	67	59	39	45	53	45	46	15
District of Columbia	65	43	80	28	48	38	57	57	41	36	33	45	67	34	66	53	58	21
Duluth, Minnesota	41	48	38	62	55	55	55	44	48	57	74	49	48	59	53	47	41	12
Elizabeth, New Jersey	42	43	50	39	48	43	43	50	46	48	51	64	44	52	63	64	51	17
Erie, Pennsylvania	47	50	44	61	62	60	47	44	52	57	80	53	41	59	41	50	41	12
Evansville, Indiana	47	50	46	66	55	60	47	59	64	64	57	53	50	52	53	38	49	16
Flint, Michigan	52	54	55	57	69	55	38	55	50	48	49	45	44	45	46	46	49	16
Fort Lauderdale, Florida	33	69	58	57	40	48	55	53	65	62	50	35	80	40	66	57	34	10
Fort Wayne, Indiana	49	54	47	53	62	55	53	47	44	48	40	45	53	45	41	44	43	13
Fort Worth, Texas	57	56	53	50	62	55	53	57	61	62	43	53	53	52	46	58	58	21

(continued)

Table B-2 (Continued)

City and State	1	2	3	4	5	6	7	8	9	10	11	12	13	14	15	16	17	18
						Independent Variables											Dependent Variable	
																	Raw Score	
Fresno, California	47	59	49	59	55	60	59	47	55	62	60	59	50	59	63	50	41	12
Gary, Indiana	50	57	69	70	65	67	30	72	30	36	34	62	53	80	35	41	46	15
Glendale, California	45	55	32	31	33	33	70	28	41	48	45	35	58	40	53	80	43	13
Grand Rapids, Michigan	50	47	49	53	55	55	50	41	46	57	56	49	44	52	41	56	51	17
Greensboro, North Carolina	45	63	59	43	62	60	52	55	39	48	26	55	54	40	46	47	52	18
Hammond, Indiana	43	56	40	55	62	60	36	61	36	36	40	49	58	69	35	64	56	20
Hartford, Connecticut	49	38	53	30	48	38	47	50	44	48	53	64	50	52	53	65	64	23
Houston, Texas	67	62	58	54	65	60	52	59	53	48	42	55	53	45	53	53	56	20
Huntington, West Virginia	33	43	46	62	40	48	57	47	67	68	61	55	50	52	66	40	58	21
Indianapolis, Indiana	59	51	55	46	62	52	49	57	50	48	44	45	50	52	53	53	65	24
Jackson, Mississippi	48	60	64	49	65	64	57	62	41	48	31	35	61	34	56	53	37	11
Jacksonville, Florida	52	45	72	47	55	55	39	61	62	64	51	53	63	45	63	55	70	25
Jersey City, New Jersey	55	40	52	45	48	48	43	57	46	48	70	62	39	69	53	61	61	22
Kansas City, Kansas	45	41	58	51	62	52	41	59	52	62	55	55	58	64	53	55	64	23
Kansas City, Missouri	59	49	55	41	55	43	52	50	52	57	45	45	56	59	53	57	58	21
Knoxville, Tennessee	43	36	55	55	48	52	44	28	74	74	62	67	47	59	63	41	64	23
Lansing, Michigan	42	52	46	51	62	60	53	47	41	48	46	41	41	40	53	36	43	13
Lincoln, Nebraska	46	57	40	36	62	43	66	44	36	48	41	35	60	59	35	56	41	12
Little Rock, Arkansas	42	50	59	45	48	48	61	55	55	62	38	41	56	40	63	44	49	16
Los Angeles, California	72	55	52	41	48	43	57	47	50	48	59	53	60	52	53	41	44	14

City																		
Louisville, Kentucky	58	50	55	60	62	52	43	66	61	62	56	53	47	59	72	61	72	26
Lubbock, Texas	46	64	49	57	69	64	57	70	56	62	44	59	53	59	35	65	70	25
Madison, Wisconsin	46	57	38	43	55	43	74	50	34	48	28	35	60	52	56	36	41	12
Memphis, Tennessee	60	55	66	58	62	64	47	68	53	48	40	41	61	34	53	49	46	15
Miami, Florida	55	52	56	32	33	80	43	50	74	70	64	53	64	45	56	64	52	18
Milwaukee, Wisconsin	64	52	49	45	62	48	43	50	38	48	46	49	47	59	46	49	46	15
Minneapolis, Minnesota	59	40	40	33	48	38	59	41	44	57	47	41	48	59	41	61	44	14
Mobile, Alabama	53	62	62	64	65	69	53	68	55	48	44	41	62	40	53	41	46	15
Nashville, Tennessee	50	45	68	51	55	48	36	68	70	74	51	62	54	59	72	47	74	28
New Bedford, Massachusetts	39	41	41	40	40	48	26	37	61	68	61	72	39	64	46	53	70	25
New Haven, Connecticut	48	40	53	40	48	38	46	50	55	57	53	62	53	52	56	49	58	21
New Orleans, Louisiana	62	50	66	64	55	60	49	70	57	57	45	62	53	52	63	53	52	18
New York, New York	80	45	52	36	40	38	53	57	53	48	38	64	33	45	56	51	54	19
Newark, New Jersey	58	40	63	43	55	48	28	59	62	57	62	69	39	59	59	61	61	22
Niagara Falls, New York	39	51	47	54	62	55	38	53	38	48	62	59	47	78	41	45	49	16
Oakland, California	57	43	58	43	48	43	50	47	52	57	59	53	50	62	56	39	49	16
Oklahoma City, Oklahoma	56	57	51	48	62	55	57	55	59	62	37	49	54	52	53	49	56	20
Omaha, Nebraska	55	54	49	48	62	55	55	55	38	48	36	45	60	59	41	50	46	15
Orlando, Florida	35	63	58	47	48	52	57	53	57	64	48	35	74	40	59	57	49	16
Pasadena, California	44	51	52	38	33	33	63	34	50	48	43	41	60	52	59	34	34	10
Paterson, New Jersey	48	48	53	46	48	43	33	55	63	62	64	70	39	59	46	69	49	23
Pawtucket, Rhode Island	26	47	38	39	48	52	36	41	55	62	56	59	41	45	46	33	56	23
Peoria, Illinois	39	40	49	51	55	48	49	50	59	57	50	49	47	64	41	64	46	23
Philadelphia, Pennsylvania	70	43	59	47	48	48	41	44	52	48	54	59	39	45	56	53	54	19
Phoenix, Arizona	58	70	44	64	62	67	53	59	59	57	49	49	70	59	53	61	58	21

(continued)

Table B-2 (Continued)

City and State	\multicolumn{16}{c}{Independent Variables}																Dependent Variable	Raw Score
	1	2	3	4	5	6	7	8	9	10	11	12	13	14	15	16	17	18
Pittsburgh, Pennsylvania	62	36	54	55	48	48	49	53	56	57	65	55	39	78	63	53	51	17
Portland, Oregon	57	47	43	46	40	48	59	34	48	57	54	41	54	62	53	39	32	09
Providence, Rhode Island	53	26	44	51	40	43	41	44	62	68	58	62	47	52	53	58	64	23
Reading, Pennsylvania	37	36	43	34	40	38	34	34	59	62	56	62	39	62	46	45	61	22
Richmond, Virginia	54	43	74	43	48	48	49	57	50	48	33	49	50	34	66	61	61	22
Riverside, California	33	64	44	59	55	67	69	44	41	57	51	45	64	52	53	34	30	08
Rochester, New York	56	43	47	44	48	38	44	41	48	57	55	59	41	52	53	69	51	17
Rockford, Illinois	46	58	43	47	62	55	50	47	38	48	41	49	54	45	46	74	56	20
Sacramento, California	52	58	46	36	48	48	68	44	41	48	58	49	53	59	56	38	41	12
St. Louis, Missouri	65	31	61	50	55	43	41	66	57	62	46	55	44	59	59	49	74	28
St. Paul, Minnesota	56	47	41	48	55	52	55	50	39	48	47	45	47	62	41	32	41	12
St. Petersburg, Florida	50	65	52	80	26	28	55	41	66	80	48	41	74	45	56	47	41	12
Salt Lake City, Utah	51	49	38	50	55	60	66	53	50	57	43	41	56	59	59	44	51	17
San Antonio, Texas	62	59	47	74	69	69	50	80	69	70	54	80	48	69	56	44	65	24
San Bernardino, California	36	59	49	67	62	64	61	50	46	57	60	53	60	64	53	45	41	12
San Francisco, California	64	43	50	26	33	31	61	41	50	48	56	53	53	59	59	38	51	17
San Jose, California	53	66	38	58	69	52	57	47	48	48	65	55	63	59	53	39	49	16
Santa Ana, California	38	68	40	62	65	60	50	55	57	57	56	49	65	69	63	45	56	20
Schenectady, New York	30	36	41	52	40	43	55	34	59	62	72	55	41	52	46	66	43	13
Scranton, Pennsylvania	43	32	38	59	40	48	46	41	64	64	66	62	33	59	63	57	43	13

City																		
Seattle, Washington	61	53	44	38	40	48	68	37	39	48	57	41	56	59	56	41	37	11
Shreveport, Louisiana	49	56	63	55	62	64	52	62	53	48	43	45	61	34	59	55	44	14
South Bend, Indiana	47	51	50	52	55	60	52	47	32	48	42	45	50	45	35	40	41	12
Spokane, Washington	51	51	38	59	55	55	63	44	41	62	66	41	60	59	53	38	41	12
Springfield, Massachusetts	50	50	49	50	55	52	50	44	44	57	56	55	47	52	46	64	49	16
Syracuse, New York	54	45	44	45	48	43	55	41	48	48	48	53	44	52	53	69	46	15
Tacoma, Washington	48	48	43	60	48	60	50	41	50	62	62	45	53	69	41	36	46	15
Tampa, Florida	55	68	54	56	48	55	46	53	66	68	54	55	65	52	56	57	54	19
Toledo, Ohio	56	49	52	54	55	52	47	44	48	57	59	49	44	59	46	47	44	14
Topeka, Kansas	45	61	49	52	65	48	63	53	44	57	38	41	58	59	72	56	56	20
Torrance, California	38	72	32	68	69	74	59	53	28	28	50	35	62	45	46	30	32	09
Trenton, New Jersey	44	36	56	46	40	43	39	47	53	57	51	69	44	62	74	61	54	19
Tucson, Arizona	53	74	41	69	62	64	55	61	59	57	57	49	70	62	53	51	51	17
Tulsa, Oklahoma	55	59	49	50	55	60	66	47	48	57	45	41	58	40	46	44	43	13
Utica, New York	38	47	41	53	48	43	50	37	55	57	69	62	33	52	72	56	44	14
Waterbury, Connecticut	41	48	47	43	48	52	39	50	34	36	61	67	33	52	35	74	51	17
Wichita, Kansas	54	61	49	51	65	60	61	53	48	48	50	41	58	45	46	61	52	18
Wilmington, Delaware	36	28	59	43	48	48	41	47	56	57	55	59	47	52	46	62	54	19
Winston-Salem, North Carolina	43	55	66	51	62	60	44	61	44	48	31	55	56	34	56	55	51	17
Worcester, Massachusetts	51	38	38	52	40	48	49	41	48	57	48	59	41	52	53	74	52	18
Yonkers, New York	51	55	43	45	48	48	63	50	36	36	42	53	39	45	53	58	37	11
Youngstown, Ohio	49	47	55	65	55	52	38	53	50	48	60	64	41	78	46	44	37	11

Key to Table B-3: T Score For Independent and Dependent Variables
Used In Nonwhite Dropout Regression For 131 Sample Cities

1. Population Per Square Mile

2. Total Population in 1960

3. Percent Nonwhite in 1950

4. Percent Nonwhite, Non-Negro in 1960

5. Nonworker Ratio

6. Percent of Total Employed Civilian Labor Force in White Collar
   Occupations

7. Percent of Nonwhite Families with Income Under $1,000

8. Percent of Nonwhite Families with Income of $10,000 or More

9. Percent of Nonwhite Civilian Labor Force 14 Years and Over
   Who Are Unemployed

10. Percent of Nonwhite Population 25 Years and Over Who Com-
    pleted Less than Five Years of School (Nonwhite Adult Functional
    Illiteracy Rate)

11. Percent of Nonwhite Employed Population Who Are Operatives
    and Kindred Workers

12. Percent of Nonwhite Employed Population Who Are Service Work-
    ers, Except Private Household

13. Percent of Nonwhite Employed Population Who Are Laborers,
    Except Farm and Mine

14. Percent of Nonwhite Females Aged 14-65 Not in the Labor Force,
    Not in School, Not Inmates of an Institution, with Children Under
    6, Husband Not Present

15. White Dropout Rate

16. Median Rent

17. Nonwhite Dropout Rate - T Score

18. Nonwhite Dropout Rate - Percent

Table B-3
T Score For Independent And Dependent Variables Used In Nonwhite Dropout Regression For 131 Sample Cities

City and State	Independent Variables																	Dependent Variable	Raw Score
	1	2	3	4	5	6	7	8	9	10	11	12	13	14	15	16	17	18	19
Akron, Ohio	51	55	52	46	55	43	45	55	62	53	72	48	49	50	41	46	52	49	25
Albany, New York	55	47	46	51	43	59	58	49	49	48	49	54	54	42	56	51	45	46	23
Albuquerque, New Mexico	42	52	41	62	62	74	45	62	39	43	39	54	51	52	46	49	64	55	29
Allentown, Pennsylvania	53	42	37	46	41	42	34	34	34	34	34	34	34	35	53	51	48	47	24
Anaheim, California	45	40	37	59	66	61	34	34	34	34	34	34	34	35	35	41	74	46	23
Atlanta, Georgia	44	59	70	34	47	49	53	49	37	63	54	61	53	40	66	58	44	50	26
Austin, Texas	44	51	55	51	58	66	61	45	43	56	43	70	49	50	63	58	43	45	22
Baltimore, Maryland	62	68	60	54	50	43	51	59	56	56	55	44	57	50	63	70	56	56	30
Baton Rouge, Louisiana	49	48	62	54	61	55	55	45	58	74	51	54	61	42	53	41	41	44	21
Beaumont, Texas	32	45	62	46	60	47	70	45	49	74	51	48	69	40	56	44	40	45	22
Berkeley, California	61	43	56	74	36	80	38	69	52	40	41	45	45	42	53	30	62	31	08
Birmingham, Alabama	47	57	72	46	60	46	70	45	56	68	62	45	63	42	59	56	32	50	26
Boston, Massachusetts	65	63	47	59	38	49	51	55	47	41	54	56	38	68	59	61	58	62	35
Bridgeport, Connecticut	59	49	46	46	44	36	53	59	58	48	61	41	45	65	41	56	55	61	34
Buffalo, New York	64	61	50	57	53	41	51	52	67	51	61	41	61	59	56	51	49	57	31
Cambridge, Massachusetts	70	42	47	61	38	59	41	72	37	37	48	47	35	50	56	54	59	40	18
Camden, New Jersey	64	44	55	55	59	33	53	55	49	53	62	45	49	59	41	61	44	53	28
Canton, Ohio	57	44	48	46	57	39	58	52	67	53	58	38	69	50	41	52	47	50	26

City																		
Charleston, West Virginia	38	34	46	54	66	63	45	43	52	39	67	42	42	63	49	49	50	26
Charlotte, North Carolina	39	52	46	44	52	53	45	43	66	52	55	58	50	46	51	49	56	30
Chattanooga, Tennessee	41	47	34	58	38	70	45	47	68	53	57	62	50	63	61	33	50	26
Chicago, Illinois	68	74	59	37	46	45	64	59	50	54	47	43	61	56	54	69	53	28
Cincinnati, Ohio	53	61	51	55	42	58	52	58	58	45	51	61	59	53	70	45	53	28
Cleveland, Ohio	61	66	54	48	33	51	62	59	50	59	43	53	52	53	61	59	53	28
Clifton, New Jersey	55	30	46	39	52	34	34	34	34	34	34	34	35	26	37	65	30	00
Columbia, South Carolina	50	37	46	64	61	80	45	39	68	45	56	54	50	80	49	36	47	24
Columbus, Ohio	50	59	51	52	50	51	59	56	48	51	54	51	55	72	64	62	53	28
Corpus Christi, Texas	47	50	46	72	52	67	39	47	63	57	59	59	40	41	64	36	53	28
Dallas, Texas	35	63	54	41	57	55	45	43	56	49	62	55	42	46	61	52	63	35
Davenport, Iowa	33	35	46	52	50	61	39	52	40	58	45	59	72	53	49	55	47	24
Dayton, Ohio	56	55	46	49	43	51	62	49	48	53	50	49	55	46	56	62	49	25
Dearborn, Michigan	47	43	46	52	63	34	34	34	34	34	34	34	35	41	26	67	30	00
Denver, Colorado	55	60	61	47	63	45	62	43	38	42	61	44	55	46	58	52	44	21
Des Moines, Iowa	40	53	54	45	66	51	52	49	43	44	61	53	69	46	51	52	49	25
Detroit, Michigan	62	69	54	53	43	58	59	69	48	65	41	44	52	53	46	57	45	22
District of Columbia	63	65	60	28	57	41	68	43	45	53	54	45	46	66	58	62	53	28
Duluth, Minnesota	32	41	57	62	55	58	52	74	37	44	69	36	80	53	41	41	57	31
Elizabeth, New Jersey	59	42	46	39	43	41	59	56	56	70	43	44	61	63	51	59	64	36
Erie, Pennsylvania	56	47	46	61	47	67	49	80	58	51	36	59	59	41	41	48	50	26
Evansville, Indiana	47	47	59	66	47	74	39	58	58	51	66	54	52	53	49	40	38	15
Flint, Michigan	54	52	51	57	38	45	59	64	45	80	41	39	40	46	49	62	46	23
Fort Lauderdale, Florida	44	33	51	57	55	55	45	39	66	46	48	74	40	66	34	67	57	31
Fort Wayne, Indiana	47	49	51	53	53	55	55	58	51	59	54	49	50	41	43	55	44	21

(continued)

Table B-3 (Continued)

City and State	\ 1	2	3	4	5	6	7	8	9	10	11	12	13	14	15	16	17	18	19
						Independent Variables												*Dependent Variable*	*Raw Score*
Fort Worth, Texas	36	57	55	51	50	53	61	39	47	56	51	61	59	46	46	58	43	58	33
Fresno, California	48	47	50	65	59	59	58	52	62	52	39	54	46	59	63	41	48	50	26
Gary, Indiana	46	50	62	46	70	30	45	59	47	50	58	35	63	46	35	46	55	41	20
Glendale, California	45	45	31	57	31	70	34	34	34	34	34	34	34	35	53	43	62	80	63
Grand Rapids, Michigan	56	50	46	54	53	50	51	49	64	50	59	54	51	59	41	51	48	56	30
Greensboro, North Carolina	36	45	61	51	43	52	51	49	35	59	51	51	57	42	46	52	49	47	24
Hammond, Indiana	48	43	37	46	55	36	51	55	47	56	59	39	65	46	35	56	64	64	36
Hartford, Connecticut	59	49	50	51	30	47	45	52	56	50	57	43	53	67	53	64	62	65	38
Houston, Texas	37	67	59	54	54	52	58	49	47	56	53	54	59	40	53	56	47	53	28
Huntington, West Virginia	53	33	47	34	62	57	67	45	43	59	36	74	51	50	66	58	43	40	18
Indianapolis, Indiana	54	59	56	46	46	49	51	59	52	48	52	51	53	46	53	65	57	53	28
Jackson, Mississippi	39	48	74	34	49	57	61	39	43	61	57	50	55	46	56	37	36	53	28
Jacksonville, Florida	54	52	68	46	47	39	58	45	43	66	52	47	65	46	63	70	41	55	29
Jersey City, New Jersey	74	55	50	51	45	43	41	55	52	52	65	43	55	59	53	61	50	61	34
Kansas City, Kansas	38	45	59	46	51	41	51	52	52	50	54	55	57	50	53	64	47	55	29
Kansas City, Missouri	43	59	53	51	41	52	53	52	52	45	46	56	49	55	53	58	47	57	31
Knoxville, Tennessee	47	43	56	51	55	44	67	45	47	61	41	74	51	55	63	64	32	41	19
Lansing, Michigan	50	42	43	51	51	53	45	62	49	41	63	50	41	59	53	43	59	36	13
Lincoln, Nebraska	50	46	37	55	36	66	36	49	47	35	43	63	41	52	35	41	53	56	30
Little Rock, Arkansas	44	42	60	34	45	61	61	39	39	56	49	57	55	50	63	49	41	44	21

City																		
Los Angeles, California	72	53	68	41	57	41	65	52	41	48	48	41	50	53	44	58	41	19
Louisville, Kentucky	58	58	46	60	43	63	45	56	58	48	59	57	52	72	72	41	61	34
Lubbock, Texas	46	52	46	57	57	53	49	39	56	49	59	64	46	35	70	47	65	40
Madison, Wisconsin	46	37	59	43	74	51	64	37	35	35	56	36	37	56	41	72	36	13
Memphis, Tennessee	60	70	46	58	47	67	39	47	63	61	48	59	50	53	46	37	49	25
Miami, Florida	55	58	51	32	43	51	39	52	59	48	56	61	40	56	52	58	64	36
Milwaukee, Wisconsin	64	46	57	45	43	45	62	59	48	68	39	51	63	46	46	68	49	25
Minneapolis, Minnesota	59	41	59	33	59	51	59	49	40	42	63	41	65	41	44	57	61	34
Mobile, Alabama	53	68	46	64	53	63	45	56	61	55	45	69	50	53	46	26	41	20
Nashville, Tennessee	50	63	46	51	36	67	45	39	59	51	62	55	46	72	74	32	47	24
New Bedford, Massachusetts	39	43	54	40	26	67	55	62	56	74	44	39	72	46	70	38	53	28
New Haven, Connecticut	48	48	55	40	46	51	52	56	45	63	47	43	67	56	58	55	49	25
New Orleans, Louisiana	62	64	51	64	49	58	45	52	63	52	48	64	52	63	52	40	53	28
New York, New York	80	52	59	36	53	41	59	72	45	53	54	39	52	56	54	53	51	27
Newark, New Jersey	58	58	54	43	28	51	59	59	51	63	41	49	50	59	61	57	61	34
Niagara Falls, New York	39	46	57	54	38	53	59	59	56	55	37	70	61	41	49	62	45	22
Oakland, California	57	56	70	43	50	45	62	64	50	45	45	54	59	46	49	53	39	16
Oklahoma City, Oklahoma	56	52	65	44	57	61	43	43	45	44	54	51	63	53	56	41	49	25
Omaha, Nebraska	55	50	55	48	55	45	47	47	43	59	58	51	55	41	46	55	50	26
Orlando, Florida	35	61	51	47	57	51	39	47	69	43	50	80	37	59	49	57	57	31
Pasadena, California	44	52	67	38	63	51	59	43	38	41	50	45	61	59	34	59	34	11
Paterson, New Jersey	48	48	51	46	33	51	49	62	56	68	36	53	59	46	64	55	69	44
Pawtucket, Rhode Island	26	31	46	39	36	34	34	34	34	34	34	34	35	46	64	38	33	13
Peoria, Illinois	39	47	51	51	49	61	45	49	53	53	57	51	59	41	64	48	64	36
Philadelphia, Pennsylvania	70	59	54	47	41	51	55	58	51	55	47	49	52	56	54	44	53	28

(continued)

Table B-3 (Continued)

City and State	1	2	3	4	5	6	7	8	9	10	11	12	13	14	15	16	17	18	19
	Independent Variables (T Score)																	Dependent Variable (T Score)	Raw Score (Dependent Variable)
Phoenix, Arizona	34	58	48	61	64	53	53	52	52	58	41	51	59	55	53	58	55	61	34
Pittsburgh, Pennsylvania	61	62	53	46	55	49	53	52	66	52	46	58	58	55	63	51	48	53	28
Portland, Oregon	51	57	46	65	46	59	41	55	56	50	38	64	46	59	53	32	50	39	16
Providence, Rhode Island	62	53	46	57	51	41	58	45	56	45	52	50	44	63	53	64	40	58	32
Reading, Pennsylvania	60	37	43	46	34	34	63	45	58	61	64	45	62	59	46	61	37	45	22
Richmond, Virginia	52	54	64	51	43	49	58	49	47	61	57	55	53	46	66	61	48	61	34
Riverside, California	34	33	47	57	59	69	35	55	47	38	49	50	42	46	53	30	62	34	11
Rochester, New York	59	56	41	51	44	44	51	55	64	56	49	50	57	59	53	51	58	69	44
Rockford, Illinois	49	46	43	46	47	50	53	62	62	51	57	51	46	59	46	56	65	74	45
Sacramento, California	46	52	50	72	36	68	35	72	49	50	39	44	44	50	56	41	52	38	14
St. Louis, Missouri	63	65	59	51	50	41	58	52	52	53	49	54	53	59	59	74	45	49	25
St. Paul, Minnesota	53	56	41	55	48	55	45	62	56	37	43	72	38	59	41	41	53	32	10
St. Petersburg, Florida	41	50	56	34	80	55	58	45	43	59	48	50	65	37	56	41	52	47	24
Salt Lake City, Utah	41	51	41	63	50	66	38	68	37	43	41	61	37	55	59	51	47	44	21
San Antonio, Texas	43	62	50	54	74	50	55	45	43	52	46	66	43	46	56	65	32	44	21
San Bernardino, California	42	36	43	57	67	61	45	49	64	48	51	50	53	63	53	41	48	45	22
San Francisco, California	66	64	53	80	26	61	38	68	56	58	39	61	42	52	59	51	53	38	14
San Jose, California	43	53	41	66	58	57	36	74	49	45	45	41	39	37	53	49	70	39	16
Santa Ana, California	48	38	37	60	62	50	45	59	66	41	35	59	57	42	63	56	64	45	22
Schenectady, New York	57	30	41	51	52	55	61	52	59	48	45	57	53	37	46	43	47	66	43

Location																			
Scranton, Pennsylvania	47	43	37	46	59	46	34	34	34	34	34	34	34	35	63	43	36	57	31
Seattle, Washington	53	61	48	70	38	68	41	68	58	45	41	54	42	50	56	37	55	41	20
Shreveport, Louisiana	47	49	65	46	55	52	61	39	47	80	53	58	61	55	59	44	36	55	29
South Bend, Indiana	51	47	50	46	52	52	55	52	56	48	70	44	46	55	35	41	55	40	18
Spokane, Washington	45	51	41	62	59	63	38	59	66	48	38	66	49	50	53	41	43	38	14
Springfield, Massachusetts	50	50	46	51	50	50	41	59	56	43	61	41	49	52	46	49	53	64	37
Syracuse, New York	58	54	41	57	45	55	51	52	56	53	53	47	49	55	53	46	59	69	44
Tacoma, Washington	39	48	43	63	60	50	51	52	72	41	45	54	55	63	41	46	43	36	13
Tampa, Florida	40	55	59	46	56	46	61	45	43	70	48	43	69	46	56	54	40	57	31
Toledo, Ohio	54	56	50	46	54	47	55	49	69	52	59	50	51	55	46	44	49	47	24
Topeka, Kansas	41	45	50	57	52	63	51	55	49	44	44	69	46	61	72	56	55	56	30
Torrance, California	50	38	43	65	68	59	38	80	35	40	37	35	35	35	46	32	80	30	00
Trenton, New Jersey	66	44	53	46	46	39	53	59	52	53	61	47	53	55	74	54	55	61	34
Tucson, Arizona	38	53	50	62	69	55	53	49	52	59	37	62	57	46	53	51	55	51	27
Tulsa, Oklahoma	51	55	52	65	50	66	61	49	49	48	41	64	49	65	46	43	47	44	21
Utica, New York	52	38	41	46	53	50	72	49	62	63	65	37	45	74	72	44	43	56	30
Waterbury, Connecticut	44	41	46	46	43	39	45	63	66	48	68	39	44	59	35	51	47	74	45
Wichita, Kansas	49	54	47	57	51	61	51	49	52	43	52	63	44	65	46	52	52	61	34
Wilmington, Delaware	53	36	58	51	43	41	51	55	56	53	49	44	58	55	46	54	52	62	35
Winston-Salem, North Carolina	42	43	80	34	51	44	63	45	52	66	64	50	57	55	56	51	43	55	29
Worcester, Massachusetts	49	51	37	46	52	49	41	45	49	43	57	57	42	67	53	52	49	74	45
Yonkers, New York	60	51	43	51	45	63	65	65	47	41	55	41	42	46	53	37	64	58	33
Youngstown, Ohio	49	55	55	46	65	38	55	49	62	58	55	39	72	42	46	37	52	44	21

Key to Table B-4: Score For Independent And Dependent Variables Used In White Adult Functional Illiteracy Regression For 131 Sample Cities

1. Increase in Total Population 1950-1960

2. Fertility Ratio

3. Nonworker Ratio

4. Percent of Total Population Under 5 Years of Age

5. Percent of Total Employed Civilian Labor Force in White Collar Occupations

6. Percent of Occupied Units with 1.01 or More Persons Per Room

7. Percent of White Families with Income Under $1,000

8. Percent of White Population 5 Years Old and Over in 1960 Who Lived in a Different State in 1955

9. Percent of White Male Employed Population Who Are Professional, Technical and Kindred Workers

10. Percent of White Male Employed Population Who Are Service Workers, Except Private Household

11. Percent of White Male Employed Population Who Are Laborers, Except Farm and Mine

12. Ratio of Males Aged 35-44 to Females Aged 35-44

13. Percent of Males 35-44 Not in Labor Force

14. Median Rent

15. White Adult Functional Illiteracy Rate - T Score

16. White Adult Functional Illiteracy Rate - Percent

Table B-4
T Score For Independent And Dependent Variables Used In White Adult Functional Illiteracy Regression For 131 Sample Cities

| City and State | T Score | | | | | | | | | | | | | | | Raw Score |
| | Independent Variables | | | | | | | | | | | | | | Dependent Variable | |
	1	2	3	4	5	6	7	8	9	10	11	12	13	14	15	16
Akron, Ohio	50	57	55	55	43	47	41	47	49	45	52	50	41	52	49	05
Albany, New York	43	43	43	48	59	37	59	39	55	68	62	38	56	45	53	06
Albuquerque, New Mexico	65	68	62	69	74	61	48	68	69	52	52	64	46	64	49	05
Allentown, Pennsylvania	47	37	41	40	42	34	44	39	44	58	62	48	53	48	49	05
Anaheim, California	80	67	66	69	61	47	44	67	64	45	45	74	35	74	35	02
Atlanta, Georgia	60	46	47	55	49	66	57	56	55	39	40	41	66	44	53	06
Austin, Texas	58	50	58	55	66	59	62	48	66	58	52	54	63	43	67	11
Baltimore, Maryland	47	50	50	55	43	53	55	44	52	52	52	55	63	56	59	08
Baton Rouge, Louisiana	54	52	61	62	55	66	44	56	66	39	40	48	53	41	45	04
Beaumont, Texas	55	56	60	62	47	61	56	50	55	39	40	59	56	40	49	05
Berkeley, California	44	26	36	33	80	37	44	58	80	58	45	48	53	62	41	03
Birmingham, Alabama	49	50	60	55	46	66	52	50	49	39	40	41	59	32	45	04
Boston, Massachusetts	31	43	38	48	49	47	52	44	49	74	59	54	59	58	59	08
Bridgeport, Connecticut	45	49	44	55	36	53	56	44	41	58	52	60	41	55	62	09
Buffalo, New York	38	49	53	48	41	41	53	33	41	58	64	50	56	49	55	07
Cambridge, Massachusetts	36	34	38	40	59	44	48	61	72	72	52	43	56	59	53	06
Camden, New Jersey	41	53	59	55	33	50	61	44	32	62	59	50	41	44	67	11
Canton, Ohio	44	53	57	55	39	50	53	41	38	52	69	50	41	47	55	07

Charleston, West Virginia	52	40	54	48	66	53	64	47	61	39	52	38	63	49	53	06
Charlotte, North Carolina	60	53	44	62	52	59	46	60	49	30	34	54	46	49	49	05
Chattanooga, Tennessee	47	47	58	55	38	62	69	56	49	45	52	28	63	33	62	09
Chicago, Illinois	45	49	37	55	46	57	44	44	44	58	52	59	56	69	59	08
Cincinnati, Ohio	47	55	55	55	42	66	59	50	55	52	52	35	53	45	53	06
Cleveland, Ohio	43	54	48	62	33	53	50	48	32	52	62	59	53	59	62	09
Clifton, New Jersey	56	38	39	48	52	37	28	44	52	45	45	54	26	65	55	07
Columbia, South Carolina	51	37	64	48	61	59	59	56	64	52	40	55	80	36	53	06
Columbus, Ohio	55	60	52	62	50	53	53	53	56	45	52	64	72	62	45	04
Corpus Christi, Texas	61	72	72	69	52	74	72	48	52	52	64	55	41	36	74	17
Dallas, Texas	62	52	41	62	57	57	50	54	57	39	45	55	46	52	53	06
Davenport, Iowa	53	63	52	62	50	55	41	56	44	52	62	61	53	55	35	02
Dayton, Ohio	50	51	49	55	43	55	50	50	52	45	52	55	46	62	49	05
Dearborn, Michigan	53	33	52	40	63	41	32	26	64	52	45	43	41	67	53	06
Denver, Colorado	53	50	47	55	63	47	46	63	57	58	59	54	46	52	45	04
Des Moines, Iowa	52	50	45	55	66	50	44	50	52	52	59	54	46	52	41	03
Detroit, Michigan	37	47	53	48	43	50	50	39	49	58	45	48	53	57	59	08
District of Columbia	43	40	28	48	57	57	41	67	74	52	34	35	66	62	45	04
Duluth, Minnesota	48	56	62	55	55	44	48	48	49	58	59	54	53	41	49	05
Elizabeth, New Jersey	43	43	39	48	43	50	46	44	49	62	52	54	63	59	64	10
Erie, Pennsylvania	50	59	61	62	47	44	52	41	44	45	59	50	41	48	53	06
Evansville, Indiana	50	52	66	55	47	59	64	50	44	52	52	38	53	40	53	06
Flint, Michigan	54	80	57	69	38	55	50	44	49	39	45	67	46	62	45	04
Fort Lauderdale, Florida	69	40	57	40	55	53	65	80	49	58	40	41	66	67	35	02
Fort Wayne, Indiana	54	62	53	62	53	47	44	53	57	52	45	54	41	55	45	04

(continued)

Table B-4 (Continued)

City and State	T Score														Raw Score	
	Independent Variables														Dependent Variable	
	1	2	3	4	5	6	7	8	9	10	11	12	13	14	15	16
Fort Worth, Texas	56	52	50	62	53	57	61	53	61	45	52	55	46	43	53	06
Fresno, California	59	51	59	55	59	47	55	50	52	62	59	59	63	48	59	08
Gary, Indiana	57	69	70	65	30	72	30	53	41	45	80	69	35	55	62	09
Glendale, California	55	28	31	33	70	28	41	58	61	52	40	41	53	62	35	02
Grand Rapids, Michigan	47	59	53	55	50	41	46	44	49	52	52	45	41	48	49	05
Greensboro, North Carolina	63	45	43	62	52	55	39	54	49	30	40	60	46	49	55	07
Hammond, Indiana	56	60	55	62	36	61	36	58	38	39	69	67	35	64	49	05
Hartford, Connecticut	38	46	30	48	47	50	44	50	41	68	52	60	53	62	64	10
Houston, Texas	62	61	54	65	52	59	53	53	59	39	45	67	53	47	55	07
Huntington, West Virginia	43	36	62	40	57	47	67	50	52	45	52	41	66	43	55	07
Indianapolis, Indiana	51	62	46	62	49	57	50	50	52	52	52	50	53	57	45	04
Jackson, Mississippi	60	59	49	65	57	62	41	61	64	39	34	45	56	36	35	02
Jacksonville, Florida	45	50	47	55	39	61	62	63	41	45	45	35	63	41	53	06
Jersey City, New Jersey	40	44	45	48	43	57	46	39	38	68	69	48	53	50	62	09
Kansas City, Kansas	41	61	51	62	41	59	52	58	32	52	64	45	53	47	55	07
Kansas City, Missouri	49	51	41	55	52	50	52	56	49	52	59	48	53	47	45	04
Knoxville, Tennessee	36	38	55	48	44	28	74	47	49	45	59	28	63	32	67	11
Lansing, Michigan	52	62	51	62	53	47	41	41	52	58	40	50	53	59	41	03
Lincoln, Nebraska	57	55	36	62	66	44	36	60	61	58	59	64	35	53	35	02
Little Rock, Arkansas	50	41	45	48	61	55	55	56	59	39	40	31	63	41	41	03

City																
Los Angeles, California	55	45	41	48	57	47	50	60	64	52	52	61	53	58	53	06
Louisville, Kentucky	50	57	60	62	43	66	61	47	44	45	59	50	72	41	53	06
Lubbock, Texas	64	65	57	69	57	70	56	53	49	45	59	72	35	47	59	08
Madison, Wisconsin	57	48	43	55	74	50	34	60	72	68	52	64	56	72	35	02
Memphis, Tennessee	55	59	58	62	47	68	53	61	49	39	34	45	53	37	41	03
Miami, Florida	52	30	32	33	43	50	74	64	44	80	45	48	56	58	53	06
Milwaukee, Wisconsin	52	59	45	62	43	50	38	47	44	52	59	60	46	68	49	05
Minneapolis, Minnesota	40	41	33	48	59	41	44	48	55	62	59	41	41	57	41	03
Mobile, Alabama	62	64	64	65	53	68	55	62	55	30	40	54	53	26	41	03
Nashville, Tennessee	45	48	51	55	36	68	70	54	41	52	59	38	72	32	62	09
New Bedford, Massachusetts	41	44	40	40	26	37	61	39	26	68	64	43	46	38	72	14
New Haven, Connecticut	40	44	40	48	46	50	55	53	55	62	52	50	56	55	62	09
New Orleans, Louisiana	50	54	64	55	49	70	57	53	57	58	52	45	63	40	62	09
New York, New York	45	33	36	40	53	57	53	33	52	72	45	41	56	53	64	10
Newark, New Jersey	40	47	43	55	28	59	62	39	38	68	59	50	59	57	69	12
Niagara Falls, New York	51	58	54	62	38	53	38	47	44	52	78	64	41	62	59	08
Oakland, California	43	43	43	48	50	47	52	50	52	52	62	48	46	53	53	06
Oklahoma City, Oklahoma	57	54	48	62	57	55	59	54	55	45	52	60	53	41	49	05
Omaha, Nebraska	54	63	48	62	55	55	38	60	49	52	59	59	41	55	45	04
Orlando, Florida	63	46	47	48	57	53	57	74	59	39	40	59	59	52	35	02
Pasadena, California	51	35	38	33	63	34	50	60	69	52	52	43	59	59	41	03
Paterson, New Jersey	48	46	46	48	33	55	63	39	32	58	59	54	46	55	70	13
Pawtucket, Rhode Island	47	48	39	48	36	41	55	41	38	58	45	48	46	38	59	08
Peoria, Illinois	40	51	51	55	49	50	59	47	44	58	64	50	41	48	49	05
Philadelphia, Pennsylvania	43	45	47	48	41	44	52	39	49	58	45	45	56	44	59	08

(continued)

Table B-4 (Continued)

City and State	\multicolumn{14}{c	}{T Score — Independent Variables}	\multicolumn{2}{c}{Raw Score — Dependent Variable}
	1	2	3	4	5	6	7	8	9	10	11	12	13	14	15	16
Phoenix, Arizona	70	56	64	62	53	59	59	70	52	52	59	55	53	55	49	05
Pittsburgh, Pennsylvania	36	41	55	48	49	53	56	39	49	62	78	43	63	48	55	07
Portland, Oregon	47	39	46	40	59	34	48	54	52	58	62	45	53	50	41	03
Providence, Rhode Island	26	43	51	40	41	44	62	47	44	68	52	43	53	40	62	09
Reading, Pennsylvania	36	36	34	40	34	34	59	39	38	62	62	48	46	37	62	09
Richmond, Virginia	43	39	43	48	49	57	50	50	55	45	34	38	66	48	49	05
Riverside, California	64	53	59	55	69	44	41	64	64	52	52	67	53	62	45	04
Rochester, New York	43	48	44	48	44	41	48	41	52	58	52	41	53	58	59	08
Rockford, Illinois	58	57	47	62	50	47	38	54	52	45	45	59	46	65	49	05
Sacramento, California	58	45	36	48	68	44	41	53	57	62	59	64	56	52	49	05
St. Louis, Missouri	31	54	50	55	41	66	57	44	41	58	59	30	59	45	55	07
St. Paul, Minnesota	47	56	48	55	55	50	39	47	55	58	62	41	41	53	45	04
St. Petersburg, Florida	65	41	80	26	55	41	66	74	55	52	45	35	56	52	41	03
Salt Lake City, Utah	49	55	50	55	66	53	50	56	59	62	59	54	59	47	41	03
San Antonio, Texas	59	74	74	69	50	80	69	48	44	58	69	50	56	32	80	20
San Bernardino, California	59	59	67	62	61	50	46	60	52	58	64	54	53	48	53	06
San Francisco, California	43	31	26	33	61	41	50	53	55	72	59	54	59	53	53	06
San Jose, California	66	65	58	69	57	47	48	63	61	52	59	72	53	70	55	07
Santa Ana, California	68	66	62	65	50	55	57	65	49	52	69	64	63	64	49	05
Schenectady, New York	36	43	52	40	55	34	59	41	61	62	52	41	46	47	55	07

City															
Scranton, Pennsylvania	32	36	59	40	46	41	64	33	38	58	59	38	63	36	62	09
Seattle, Washington	53	41	38	40	68	37	39	56	61	52	59	59	56	55	41	03
Shreveport, Louisiana	56	57	55	62	52	62	53	61	59	39	34	41	59	36	45	04
South Bend, Indiana	51	53	52	55	52	47	32	50	57	45	45	55	35	55	45	04
Spokane, Washington	51	55	59	55	63	44	41	60	49	58	59	59	53	43	41	03
Springfield, Massachusetts	50	58	50	55	50	44	44	47	49	58	52	59	46	53	55	07
Syracuse, New York	45	47	45	48	55	41	48	44	57	62	52	45	53	59	53	06
Tacoma, Washington	48	52	60	48	50	41	50	53	44	62	69	59	41	43	45	04
Tampa, Florida	68	48	56	48	46	53	66	65	41	52	52	48	56	40	55	07
Toledo, Ohio	49	55	54	55	47	44	48	44	44	45	59	54	46	49	49	05
Topeka, Kansas	61	64	52	65	63	53	44	58	57	52	59	69	72	55	41	03
Torrance, California	72	70	68	69	59	53	28	62	69	45	45	74	46	80	35	02
Trenton, New Jersey	36	38	46	40	39	47	53	44	44	68	62	61	74	55	69	12
Tucson, Arizona	74	59	69	62	55	61	59	70	57	58	62	54	53	55	49	05
Tulsa, Oklahoma	59	49	50	55	66	47	48	58	64	39	40	59	46	47	41	03
Utica, New York	47	47	53	48	50	37	55	33	52	68	52	50	72	43	62	09
Waterbury, Connecticut	48	48	43	48	39	50	34	33	38	58	52	50	35	47	67	11
Wichita, Kansas	61	62	51	65	61	53	48	58	61	45	45	61	46	52	41	03
Wilmington, Delaware	28	44	43	48	41	47	56	47	49	58	52	38	46	52	59	08
Winston-Salem, North Carolina	55	49	51	62	44	61	44	56	66	39	34	43	56	43	55	07
Worcester, Massachusetts	38	45	52	40	49	41	48	41	49	62	52	45	53	49	59	08
Yonkers, New York	55	43	45	48	63	50	36	39	57	52	45	45	53	64	53	06
Youngstown, Ohio	47	51	65	55	38	53	50	41	38	45	78	59	46	52	64	10

Key to Table B-5: T Score For Independent And Dependent Variables
Used in Nonwhite Adult Functional Illiteracy Regression For 131
Sample Cities

1. Population Per Square Mile

2. Increase in Total Population 1950-1960

3. Percent Nonwhite in 1960

4. Percent Nonwhite in 1950

5. Percent Nonwhite, Non-Negro in 1960

6. Fertility Ratio

7. Percent of Total Population Between 5-18 Years of Age

8. Percent of Total Employed Civilian Labor Force in White Collar
   Occupations

9. Percent of Nonwhite Families with Income Under $1,000

10. Percent of Nonwhite Families with Income Between $1,000-$1,999

11. Percent of Nonwhite Families with Income of $10,000 or More

12. Percent of Nonwhite Population 5 Years Old and Over in 1960
    Who Lived in a Different State in 1955

13. Percent of Nonwhite Male Employed Population Who Are Opera-
    tives and Kindred Workers

14. Percent of Nonwhite Male Employed Population Who Are Labor-
    ers, Except Farm and Mine

15. Percent of Nonwhite Female Employed Population Who Are Pri-
    vate Household Workers

16. Percent of Males 35-44 Not in Labor Force

17. Nonwhite Adult Illiteracy Rate - T Score

18. Nonwhite Adult Illiteracy Rate - Percent

Table B-5

T Score For Independent And Dependent Variables Used in Nonwhite Adult Functional Illiteracy Regression For For 131 Sample Cities

City and State	1	2	3	4	5	6	7	8	9	10	11	12	13	14	15	16	17	18
						Independent Variables											Dependent Variable (Raw Score)	
Akron, Ohio	51	50	51	52	46	57	55	43	45	47	55	50	72	49	53	41	53	16
Albany, New York	55	43	49	46	51	43	43	59	58	45	49	52	49	54	46	56	48	12
Albuquerque, New Mexico	42	65	41	41	62	68	67	74	45	50	62	74	39	51	55	46	43	10
Allentown, Pennsylvania	53	47	36	37	46	37	43	42	34	34	34	34	34	34	34	53	34	00
Anaheim, California	45	80	36	37	59	67	70	61	34	34	34	34	34	34	34	35	34	00
Atlanta, Georgia	44	60	68	70	34	46	52	49	53	60	49	38	54	53	59	66	63	24
Austin, Texas	44	58	51	55	51	50	55	66	61	68	45	38	43	49	65	63	56	17
Baltimore, Maryland	62	47	64	60	54	50	55	43	51	50	59	46	55	57	52	63	56	17
Baton Rouge, Louisiana	49	54	62	62	54	52	67	55	55	65	45	38	51	61	67	53	74	32
Beaumont, Texas	32	55	61	62	46	56	64	47	70	60	45	41	51	69	60	56	74	32
Berkeley, California	61	44	59	56	74	26	31	80	38	39	69	52	41	45	45	53	40	08
Birmingham, Alabama	47	49	70	72	46	50	60	46	70	62	45	38	62	63	59	59	68	27
Boston, Massachusetts	65	31	50	47	59	43	38	49	51	50	55	56	54	38	37	59	41	09
Bridgeport, Connecticut	59	45	50	46	46	49	43	36	53	47	59	59	61	45	51	41	48	12
Buffalo, New York	64	38	52	50	57	49	48	41	51	54	52	54	61	61	41	56	51	14
Cambridge, Massachusetts	70	36	45	47	61	34	28	59	41	42	72	56	48	35	38	56	37	06
Camden, New Jersey	64	41	58	55	55	53	52	33	53	45	55	47	62	49	52	41	53	16
Canton, Ohio	57	44	50	48	46	53	52	39	58	52	52	48	58	69	55	41	53	16

Charleston, West Virginia	38	52	50	52	46	40	55	66	63	62	45	44	39	42	63	63	52	15
Charlotte, North Carolina	39	60	59	62	46	53	64	52	53	60	45	47	52	58	63	46	66	26
Chattanooga, Tennessee	41	47	62	63	34	47	60	38	70	69	45	44	53	62	59	63	68	27
Chicago, Illinois	68	45	58	55	59	49	43	46	45	47	64	50	54	43	36	56	50	13
Cincinnati, Ohio	53	47	56	58	51	55	48	42	58	54	52	44	45	61	51	53	58	18
Cleveland, Ohio	61	43	61	58	54	54	48	33	51	47	62	50	59	53	44	53	50	13
Clifton, New Jersey	55	56	28	31	46	38	52	52	34	34	34	34	34	34	34	26	34	00
Columbia, South Carolina	50	51	62	68	46	37	52	61	80	74	45	41	45	54	61	80	68	27
Columbus, Ohio	50	55	54	55	51	60	48	50	51	50	59	52	51	51	49	72	48	12
Corpus Christi, Texas	47	61	45	50	46	72	74	52	67	65	39	35	57	59	70	41	63	24
Dallas, Texas	35	62	55	55	54	52	60	57	55	60	45	44	49	55	58	46	56	17
Davenport, Iowa	33	53	38	41	46	63	55	50	61	45	39	68	58	59	52	53	40	08
Dayton, Ohio	56	50	56	55	46	51	55	43	51	47	62	50	53	49	50	46	48	12
Dearborn, Michigan	47	53	28	31	46	33	64	63	34	34	34	34	34	34	34	41	34	00
Denver, Colorado	55	53	46	46	61	50	52	63	45	45	62	64	42	44	47	46	38	07
Des Moines, Iowa	40	52	43	47	54	50	52	66	51	51	52	54	44	53	47	46	43	10
Detroit, Michigan	62	37	61	58	54	47	55	43	58	52	59	44	65	44	47	53	48	12
District of Columbia	63	43	80	65	60	40	38	57	41	39	68	54	43	45	46	66	45	11
Duluth, Minnesota	32	48	36	37	57	56	55	55	58	59	52	72	44	36	44	53	37	06
Elizabeth, New Jersey	59	43	50	50	46	43	43	43	41	45	59	56	70	53	49	63	56	17
Erie, Pennsylvania	56	50	43	43	46	59	60	47	67	52	49	48	51	59	39	41	58	18
Evansville, Indiana	47	50	46	50	59	52	60	47	74	60	39	46	51	54	57	53	58	18
Flint, Michigan	54	54	55	52	51	80	55	38	45	39	59	52	80	39	49	46	45	11
Fort Lauderdale, Florida	44	69	58	60	51	40	48	55	55	54	45	58	46	74	70	66	66	26
Fort Wayne, Indiana	47	54	46	46	51	62	55	53	55	50	55	58	59	49	42	41	51	14

(continued)

Table B-5 (Continued)

| City and State | \multicolumn{16}{c}{T Score} | | | | | | | | | | | | | | | | Raw Score |
| | Independent Variables | | | | | | | | | | | | | | | | Dependent Variable | |
	1	2	3	4	5	6	7	8	9	10	11	12	13	14	15	16	17	18
Fort Worth, Texas	36	56	53	55	51	52	55	53	61	62	39	44	51	59	58	46	56	17
Fresno, California	48	59	50	50	65	51	60	59	58	50	52	48	39	46	54	63	52	15
Gary, Indiana	46	57	69	62	46	69	67	30	45	39	59	52	58	63	39	35	50	13
Glendale, California	45	55	36	31	57	28	33	70	34	34	34	34	34	34	34	53	34	00
Grand Rapids, Michigan	56	47	48	46	54	59	55	50	51	52	49	50	59	51	45	41	50	13
Greensboro, North Carolina	36	63	59	61	51	45	60	52	51	57	49	47	51	57	60	46	59	20
Hammond, Indiana	48	56	38	37	46	60	60	36	51	50	55	57	59	65	59	35	56	17
Hartford, Connecticut	59	38	53	50	51	46	38	47	45	47	52	58	57	53	49	53	50	13
Houston, Texas	37	62	57	59	54	61	60	52	58	55	49	44	53	59	57	53	56	17
Huntington, West Virginia	53	43	45	47	34	36	48	57	67	59	45	44	36	51	74	66	59	20
Indianapolis, Indiana	54	51	55	56	46	62	52	49	51	47	59	47	52	53	49	53	48	12
Jackson, Mississippi	39	60	64	74	34	59	64	57	61	72	39	38	57	55	66	56	61	22
Jacksonville, Florida	54	45	72	68	46	50	55	39	58	62	45	46	52	65	57	63	66	26
Jersey City, New Jersey	74	40	52	50	51	44	48	43	41	42	55	52	65	55	37	53	52	15
Kansas City, Kansas	38	41	57	59	46	61	52	41	51	50	52	50	54	57	45	53	50	13
Kansas City, Missouri	43	49	55	53	51	51	43	52	53	54	52	54	46	49	47	53	45	11
Knoxville, Tennessee	47	36	55	56	51	38	52	44	67	72	45	46	41	51	58	63	61	22
Lansing, Michigan	50	52	46	43	51	62	60	53	45	50	62	56	63	41	46	53	41	09
Lincoln, Nebraska	50	57	38	37	55	55	43	66	36	50	49	70	43	41	44	35	35	04
Little Rock, Arkansas	44	50	58	60	34	41	48	61	61	68	39	41	49	55	55	63	56	17

City																		
Los Angeles, California	51	55	54	53	68	45	43	57	41	42	65	62	48	41	44	53	41	09
Louisville, Kentucky	55	50	55	58	46	57	52	43	63	59	45	41	48	57	54	72	58	18
Lubbock, Texas	32	64	48	52	46	65	64	57	53	55	49	38	49	64	70	35	56	17
Madison, Wisconsin	41	57	38	37	59	48	43	74	51	50	64	80	35	36	39	56	35	05
Memphis, Tennessee	44	55	66	70	46	59	64	47	67	65	39	46	61	59	61	53	63	25
Miami, Florida	58	52	57	58	51	30	80	43	51	57	39	58	48	61	63	56	59	21
Milwaukee, Wisconsin	57	52	49	46	57	59	48	43	45	45	62	62	68	51	40	46	48	12
Minneapolis, Minnesota	58	40	41	41	59	41	38	59	51	47	59	59	42	41	38	41	40	08
Mobile, Alabama	28	62	62	68	46	64	69	53	63	62	45	41	55	69	63	53	61	23
Nashville, Tennessee	52	45	68	63	46	48	48	36	67	65	45	47	51	55	56	72	59	20
New Bedford, Massachusetts	51	41	40	43	54	44	48	26	67	50	55	41	74	39	41	46	56	17
New Haven, Connecticut	58	40	53	48	55	44	38	46	51	52	52	64	63	43	51	56	45	11
New Orleans, Louisiana	40	50	66	64	51	54	60	49	58	65	45	41	52	64	54	63	63	24
New York, New York	80	45	53	52	59	33	38	53	41	42	59	47	53	39	44	56	45	11
Newark, New Jersey	72	40	63	58	54	47	48	28	51	42	59	54	63	49	41	59	51	14
Niagara Falls, New York	56	51	48	46	57	58	55	38	53	52	59	56	55	39	49	41	56	17
Oakland, California	55	43	59	56	70	43	43	50	45	47	62	50	45	43	50	46	50	13
Oklahoma City, Oklahoma	26	57	51	52	65	54	55	57	61	59	49	46	44	51	52	53	45	11
Omaha, Nebraska	52	54	49	50	55	63	55	55	45	52	52	59	59	51	45	41	43	10
Orlando, Florida	45	63	58	61	51	46	52	57	51	68	39	61	43	80	65	59	69	28
Pasadena, California	50	51	53	52	67	35	33	63	51	42	63	62	41	45	56	59	38	07
Paterson, New Jersey	70	48	53	48	51	46	43	33	51	42	49	59	68	53	41	46	56	17
Pawtucket, Rhode Island	59	47	36	31	46	48	52	36	34	34	34	34	34	34	34	46	34	00
Peoria, Illinois	55	40	50	47	51	51	48	49	61	54	45	54	53	49	49	41	53	16
Philadelphia, Pennsylvania	67	43	59	59	54	45	48	41	51	50	55	46	55	49	49	56	51	14

(continued)

Table B-5 (Continued)

City and State	Independent Variables (T Score) 1	2	3	4	5	6	7	8	9	10	11	12	13	14	15	16	Dependent Variable 17	Raw Score 18
Phoenix, Arizona	34	70	45	48	61	56	67	53	53	59	52	57	41	59	57	53	58	18
Pittsburgh, Pennsylvania	61	36	54	53	46	41	48	49	53	55	52	41	46	58	52	63	52	15
Portland, Oregon	51	47	45	46	65	39	48	59	41	52	55	54	38	46	41	53	50	13
Providence, Rhode Island	62	26	45	46	57	43	43	41	58	59	45	48	52	44	49	53	45	11
Reading, Pennsylvania	60	36	42	43	46	36	38	34	63	45	45	46	64	62	55	46	61	22
Richmond, Virginia	52	43	74	64	51	39	48	49	58	57	49	41	57	53	52	66	61	23
Riverside, California	34	64	43	47	57	53	67	69	35	42	55	68	49	42	60	53	38	07
Rochester, New York	59	43	48	41	51	48	38	44	51	45	55	64	49	57	42	53	56	17
Rockford, Illinois	49	58	42	43	46	57	55	50	53	50	62	56	57	46	45	46	51	14
Sacramento, California	46	58	51	50	72	45	48	68	35	35	72	56	39	44	45	56	50	13
St. Louis, Missouri	63	31	61	59	51	54	43	41	58	55	52	46	49	53	49	59	53	16
St. Paul, Minnesota	53	47	41	41	55	56	52	55	45	47	62	57	43	38	36	41	37	06
St. Petersburg, Florida	41	65	51	56	34	41	28	55	58	55	45	50	48	65	65	56	59	21
Salt Lake City, Utah	41	49	38	41	63	55	60	66	38	42	68	61	41	37	41	59	43	10
San Antonio, Texas	43	59	46	50	54	74	69	50	55	62	45	46	46	43	65	56	52	15
San Bernardino, California	42	59	49	43	57	59	64	61	45	45	49	65	51	53	56	53	48	12
San Francisco, California	66	43	55	53	80	31	31	61	38	39	68	52	39	42	40	59	58	18
San Jose, California	43	66	41	41	66	65	52	57	36	37	74	61	45	39	49	53	45	11
Santa Ana, California	48	68	41	37	60	66	60	50	45	52	59	64	35	57	61	63	41	09
Schenectady, New York	57	36	41	41	51	43	43	55	61	52	52	44	45	53	53	46	48	12

City																		
Scranton, Pennsylvania	47	32	36	37	46	36	48	46	34	34	34	34	34	34	34	63	34	00
Seattle, Washington	53	53	48	48	70	41	48	68	41	37	68	57	41	42	38	56	45	11
Shreveport, Louisiana	47	56	64	65	46	57	64	52	61	74	39	38	53	61	74	59	80	34
South Bend, Indiana	51	51	50	50	46	53	60	52	55	50	52	56	70	46	54	35	48	12
Spokane, Washington	45	51	41	41	62	55	53	63	38	52	59	66	38	49	46	53	48	12
Springfield, Massachusetts	50	50	48	46	51	58	52	50	41	45	59	65	61	49	45	46	43	10
Syracuse, New York	58	45	45	41	57	47	43	55	51	42	52	62	53	49	38	53	53	16
Tacoma, Washington	39	48	43	43	63	52	60	50	51	55	52	69	45	55	49	41	41	09
Tampa, Florida	40	68	54	59	46	48	55	46	61	65	45	50	48	69	63	56	70	30
Toledo, Ohio	54	49	51	50	46	55	52	47	55	54	49	48	59	51	51	46	52	15
Topeka, Kansas	41	61	48	50	57	64	48	63	51	57	55	56	44	46	51	72	40	08
Torrance, California	50	72	36	43	65	70	74	59	38	37	80	57	37	35	35	46	40	08
Trenton, New Jersey	66	36	57	53	46	38	43	39	53	39	59	52	61	53	50	74	53	16
Tucson, Arizona	38	74	42	50	62	59	64	55	53	54	49	65	37	57	80	53	59	20
Tulsa, Oklahoma	51	59	50	52	65	49	60	66	61	60	49	46	41	49	60	46	48	12
Utica, New York	52	47	41	41	46	47	43	50	72	55	49	58	65	45	47	72	63	24
Waterbury, Connecticut	44	48	46	46	46	48	52	39	45	39	63	52	68	44	44	35	48	12
Wichita, Kansas	49	61	48	47	57	62	60	61	51	52	49	59	52	44	54	46	43	10
Wilmington, Delaware	53	28	59	58	51	44	48	41	51	55	55	50	49	58	55	46	53	16
Winston-Salem, North Carolina	42	55	66	80	34	49	60	44	63	59	45	41	64	57	55	56	66	26
Worcester, Massachusetts	49	38	36	37	46	45	48	49	41	55	45	52	57	42	51	53	43	10
Yonkers, New York	60	55	42	43	51	43	48	63	45	37	65	56	55	42	54	53	41	09
Youngstown, Ohio	49	47	55	55	46	51	52	38	55	52	49	48	55	72	53	46	58	18

Table B-6

Deviant[a] and Non-Deviant[b] Status of 131 Cities on the Four
Dependent Variables

City and State	Dependent Variables			
	Nonwhite Dropout	White Dropout	Nonwhite Adult Illiteracy	White Adult Illiteracy
Akron, Ohio				
Albany, New York				
Albuquerque, New Mexico				A
Allentown, Pennsylvania				B
Anaheim, California		A		B
Atlanta, Georgia				
Austin, Texas				A
Baltimore, Maryland		A		
Baton Rouge, Louisiana			A	
Beaumont, Texas		B	A	B
Berkeley, California			B	
Birmingham, Alabama		A		B
Boston, Massachusetts				
Bridgeport, Connecticut				
Buffalo, New York			B	B
Cambridge, Massachusetts			B	
Camden, New Jersey				
Canton, Ohio			B	B
Charleston, West Virginia				
Charlotte, North Carolina			A	A
Chattanooga, Tennessee				
Chicago, Illinois				
Cincinnati, Ohio .		A		
Cleveland, Ohio				
Clifton, New Jersey	B			A
Columbia, South Carolina				
Columbus, Ohio		A		
Corpus Christi, Texas				A
Dallas, Texas				
Davenport, Iowa	B		B	B
Dayton, Ohio				B
Dearborn, Michigan	B			
Denver, Colorado		A		
Des Moines, Iowa			B	
Detroit, Michigan			B	
District of Columbia		A		A

(continued)

Table B-6 (Continued)

City and State	Dependent Variables			
	Nonwhite Dropout	White Dropout	Nonwhite Adult Illiteracy	White Adult Illiteracy
Duluth, Minnesota				
Elizabeth, New Jersey		B		A
Erie, Pennsylvania			A	
Evansville, Indiana				
Flint, Michigan				
Fort Lauderdale, Florida		B		B
Fort Wayne, Indiana			A	
Fort Worth, Texas				
Fresno, California	A	B		
Gary, Indiana				
Glendale, California	A			
Grand Rapids, Michigan				
Greensboro, North Carolina				A
Hammond, Indiana				
Hartford, Connecticut				A
Houston, Texas				
Huntington, West Virginia	B	A		
Indianapolis, Indiana		A		
Jackson, Mississippi		B		
Jacksonville, Florida		A		
Jersey City, New Jersey		A		
Kansas City, Kansas				A
Kansas City, Missouri				
Knoxville, Tennessee		A		A
Lansing, Michigan	B			B
Lincoln, Nebraska		B		B
Little Rock, Arkansas	B			
Los Angeles, California				
Louisville, Kentucky		A		B
Lubbock, Texas		A		
Madison, Wisconsin				B
Memphis, Tennessee		B		B
Miami, Florida		B		B
Milwaukee, Wisconsin	B	B		
Minneapolis, Minnesota	A	B		B
Mobile, Alabama			B	
Nashville, Tennessee				
New Bedford, Massachusetts		A		A
New Haven, Connecticut	B			A

(continued)

Table B-6 (Continued)

City and State	Dependent Variables			
	Nonwhite Dropout	White Dropout	Nonwhite Adult Illiteracy	White Adult Illiteracy
New Orleans, Louisiana				
New York, New York				
Newark, New Jersey	A	B		
Niagara Falls, New York				
Oakland, California				
Oklahoma City, Oklahoma			B	
Omaha, Nebraska		B		
Orlando, Florida				
Pasadena, California			B	
Paterson, New Jersey			A	
Pawtucket, Rhode Island	B	A		
Peoria, Illinois	A	A		B
Philadelphia, Pennsylvania				
Phoenix, Arizona				
Pittsburgh, Pennsylvania			B	B
Portland, Oregon		B	A	
Providence, Rhode Island			B	
Reading, Pennsylvania	B			
Richmond, Virginia		A		
Riverside, California				A
Rochester, New York	A	B	A	A
Rockford, Illinois	A			
Sacramento, California			A	
St. Louis, Missouri	B	A		
St. Paul, Minnesota				
St. Petersburg, Florida				
Salt Lake City, Utah				B
San Antonio, Texas				A
San Bernardino, California				A
San Francisco, California	B		A	
San Jose, California			A	A
Santa Ana, California			B	
Schenectady, New York	A			
Scranton, Pennsylvania	A	B		
Seattle, Washington				
Shreveport, Louisiana		B	A	
South Bend, Indiana	B			
Spokane, Washington			A	
Springfield, Massachusetts	A			

(continued)

Table B-6 (Continued)

City and State	Nonwhite Dropout	White Dropout	Nonwhite Adult Illiteracy	White Adult Illiteracy
		Dependent Variables		
Syracuse, New York	A		A	
Tacoma, Washington			B	B
Tampa, Florida				
Toledo, Ohio				
Topeka, Kansas			B	
Torrance, California				
Trenton, New Jersey				
Tucson, Arizona				
Tulsa, Oklahoma			B	
Utica, New York			A	
Waterbury, Connecticut	A	A		
Wichita, Kansas	A			
Wilmington, Delaware	A			
Winston-Salem, North Carolina				
Worcester, Massachusetts	A			A
Yonkers, New York	A		B	
Youngstown, Ohio		B		

[a]Deviant "above" status is denoted by A, while deviant "below" status is denoted by B.

[b]Non-deviant status is denoted by a blank.

Teachers College · Columbia University, New York 27, N.Y.

Institute of Urban Studies

May 18, 1964

Dear Sir:

We are conducting a comparative study of premature high school withdrawal, and functional illiteracy in 131 of the largest cities in the United States, for the Social Security Administration of the United States Department of Health, Education and Welfare.

As a result of the first stage of the analysis, we were able to classify two groups of cities: those in which the dropout and/or illiteracy rates are identical with what one would expect in view of the city's social and economic conditions; and those in which the rates are much higher or lower than predicted from the analysis. In addition to reporting those cities which fall into the latter category as "exceptional" -- either in a positive or negative way -- we would like to try to uncover the factors which might be contributing to the city's "exceptional" standing.

Your city is one of the sample communities that has been found to be "exceptional." We would appreciate it greatly if you could forward to us information concerning the following:

1. High school dropout or adult education programs instituted prior to 1960.
2. Programs of expansion or reorganization of high school curriculum prior to 1960.
3. Any steps or long term programs instituted prior to 1960 that may have contributed to the overall holding power of your schools.

If there is any charge for these materials, please bill us at the above address. We hope to hear from you in the very near future, so that we will be able to explain the "exceptional" status of your city.

Thank you very much for your cooperation.

Sincerely yours,

RAD:b

Robert A. Dentler
Executive Officer

Teachers College · *Columbia University, New York 27, N. Y.*

Institute of Urban Studies

May 26, 1964

Dear Sir:

We are conducting a comparative study of premature high school withdrawal, and functional illiteracy in 131 of the largest cities in the United States, for the Social Security Administration of the United States Department of Health, Education and Welfare.

As a result of the first stage of the analysis, we were able to classify two groups of cities: those in which the dropout and/or illiteracy rates are identical with what one would expect in view of the city's social and economic conditions; and those in which the rates are much higher or lower than predicted from the analysis. In addition to reporting those cities which fall into the latter category as "exceptional" -- either in a positive or negative way -- we would like to try to uncover the factors which might be contributing to the city's "exceptional" standing.

Your city is one of the sample communities that has been found to be "exceptional". We would appreciate it greatly if you could forward to us information concerning the following:

1. Per capita city expenditures on welfare between the years <u>1955-1960</u>.
2. Average city payment per family for Aid to Families with Dependent Children between the years <u>1955-1960</u>.
3. Any steps or long term programs instituted by your department, <u>prior to 1960</u>, aimed at reducing dependency.
4. Any welfare or social services developed in your department, <u>prior to 1960</u>, that are connected with or require the cooperation of the school system.

If there is any charge for these materials, please bill us at the above address. We hope to hear from you in the very near future, so that we will be able to explain the "exceptional" status of your city.

Thank you very much for your cooperation.

Sincerely yours,

RAD:b

Robert A. Dentler

REFERENCES

Boulding, K. *Reflections on Poverty*. Official proceedings of the National Social Welfare Forum, 1961.

Brooks, D. J. *A Study to Determine the Literacy Level of Able-Bodied Persons Receiving Public Assistance*. Chicago: Cook County Department of Public Aid, 1962.

Brooks, D. J. *First They Must Read: A Study to Determine the Literacy Level of Able-Bodied Persons Receiving Public Assistance in East St. Louis, Illinois*. Illinois: Cook County Department of Public Aid, 1964.

Clark, H. F. *Classrooms in the Factory*. New York: New York University Press, 1958.

Edwards, A. L. *Statistical Methods for the Behavioral Sciences*. New York: Rinehart & Company, Inc., 1960.

Ezekiel, M. *Methods of Correlation Analysis*. New York: John Wiley & Sons, Inc., 1930.

Gans, H. J. "Some Proposals for Government Policy in an Automating Society." *The Correspondent,* January-February, 1964, 30.

Guilford, J. P. *Fundamental Statistics in Psychology and Education*. New York: McGraw-Hill Book Company, Inc., 1956.

Johnson, V. A., & Sagert, W. F. *Second Dropout Study Based on Pupils Who Entered the Ninth Grade in the Saint Paul Public Schools in September 1955*. St. Paul, Minnesota: Office of Secondary and Vocational Education St. Paul Public Schools, 1961.

Miller, S. M., Saleem, Betty L., & Herrington, B. *School Dropouts: A Commentary and Annotated Bibliography.* Syracuse, New York: Syracuse University Youth Development Center, 1964.

Mueller, J. H., & Schuessler, K. F. *Statistical Reasoning in Sociology.* Boston: Houghton Mifflin Company, 1961.

Nachman, L. R., Getson, R. F., & Odgeis, J. G. *Pilot Study of Ohio High School Dropouts 1961-1962.* Columbus, Ohio: State Department of Education, 1963.

President's Advisory Committee on Labor-Management Policy. *Automation: The benefits and problems incident to automation and other technological advances.* Washington, D.C.: U. S. Government Printing Office, 1962.

Saleem, Betty L., & Miller, S. M. *The Neglected Dropout: The Returnee.* Syracuse, New York: Syracuse University Youth Development Center, 1963.

Schiffman, J. "Employment of High School Graduates and Dropouts in 1961." *Monthly Labor Review,* May 1962, Special Labor Force Report, No. 21.

Schreiber, D. *Holding Power/Large City School Systems.* Washington, D.C.: National Education Association, 1964.

Segal, D., & Schwarm, O. J. *Retention in High Schools and Large Cities.* Washington, D.C.: U. S. Office of Education, 1957, No. 15.

Sofokidis, Jeanette, & Sullivan, Eugenia. "A New Look at School Dropouts." *Health, Education, and Welfare Indicators,* April 1964.

Tannenbaum, A. *Dropout Versus Diploma. Urban Problems Series.* New York: Teachers College Bureau of Publications, 1965, in press.

U. S. Department of Commerce, Bureau of the Census. *Compendium of City Government Finances in 1960.* Washington, D.C.: U. S. Government Printing Office, 1961.

U. S. Department of Health, Education, and Welfare. *Annual Health Education and Welfare Trends, 1961.* Washington, D.C.: U. S. Government Printing Office, 1962.

U. S. Department of Health, Education, and Welfare, Office of Education. *Current Expenditures Per Pupil in Large Public School Systems 1959-1960.* Washington, D.C.: U. S. Government Printing Office, 1962.

U. S. Department of Health, Education, and Welfare, Welfare Administration, Bureau of Family Services. *Public Assistance in the Counties of the United States: June 1960.* Washington, D.C.: Author, 1963.

Zelditch, M., Jr. *A Basic Course in Sociological Statistics.* New York: Henry Holt & Company, 1959.

Ziegler, J., Associates. *A Report of a Study of the Chicago Literacy Program.* Waperville, Illinois: Author, April 1963.